BELIEVE YOU'RE MADE FOR MORE

Praise for
BELIEVE YOU'RE MADE FOR MORE

'I love how real this book is. Natasha doesn't talk down to you or pretend change happens overnight. She meets you right where you are – with no shame, no fluff, and no judgment – and walks you forward with clear steps and deep compassion. If low self-esteem has been the invisible block holding you back, this book is your breakthrough.'

DENISE DUFFIELD-THOMAS, MONEY MINDSET MENTOR, COACH, AND BEST-SELLING AUTHOR

'Natasha's compassionate voice shines through every page, offering hope and clear steps to the self-belief we all deserve. This book is a gentle but powerful companion for anyone ready to overcome self-doubt and step into their true worth.'

DAVID R. HAMILTON, PhD, BEST-SELLING AUTHOR OF *THE JOY OF ACTUALLY GIVING A F*CK*

'This is a wonderful and important book, and I'm delighted to see it published. Natasha, whose own journey is testament to the power of the pathway she presents in Believe You're Made for More, *is a voice of hope and the possibility of healing and transformation for the many who exist outside of typical self-help circles. For those ready for change, this book is a lighthouse as to how.'*

JESSICA HUIE, MBE, ENTREPRENEUR AND AUTHOR OF *PURPOSE*

'You are very lucky to hold this book in your hands. As someone who had a traumatic start in life, I suffered from low self-esteem well into adulthood. I wish Believe You're Made for More *had already existed back then. It's beautifully written and full of practical tools. Natasha's wisdom and professionalism shine through in every word and will change your life forever.'*

YAMILE YEMOONYAH, AWARD-WINNING AUTHOR, SPIRIT GUIDE MEDIUM, AND SOUL ALIGNMENT COACH

'If you're trying to manifest your dream life but secretly don't believe you deserve it, this book is for you. Believe You're Made for More is like therapy in paperback, helping you heal low self-esteem, stop people-pleasing, and finally step into your power.'

FRANCESCA AMBER, HOST OF THE UK'S NO.1 SELF-HELP PODCAST *LAW OF ATTRACTION SAVED MY LIFE* AND SUNDAY TIMES BEST-SELLING AUTHOR OF *MANIFEST LIKE A MOTHER*

'If you know you want more but you're holding yourself back, this brilliant book is for you. If you're someone that questions your own worth, Natasha will show you that self-esteem and mindset are the foundations of having the life you really want. It's such an empowering read!'

LISA JOHNSON, BUSINESS STRATEGIST AND AUTHOR OF *MAKE MONEY ONLINE*

'Natasha's delicious, judgment-free book and her own personal "brave shares" leave you feeling safe enough to go on your own self-discovery journey with her. A practical and actionable book you'll buy for all of your friends!'

HOLLY MATTHEWS, AUTHOR OF *FIND YOUR CONFIDENCE* AND FOUNDER OF THE HAPPY ME PROJECT

'If you think something is missing in your life, it's probably more of the real you! In her brilliant new book, Natasha gives you seven clear steps to help you become your most authentic self.'

ROBERT HOLDEN, AUTHOR OF *SHIFT HAPPENS, HIGHER PURPOSE,* AND *BECOMING YOURSELF*

BELIEVE YOU'RE MADE FOR MORE

7 steps to transform low self-esteem

NATASHA PAGE

HAY HOUSE

Carlsbad, California • New York City
London • Sydney • New Delhi

Published in the United Kingdom by:
Hay House UK Ltd, 1st Floor, Crawford Corner,
91–93 Baker Street, London W1U 6QQ
Tel: +44 (0)20 3927 7290; www.hayhouse.co.uk

Text © Natasha Page, 2026

The VITALS exercise on pages 100–104 has been adapted from © Meg Selig: www.psychologytoday.com/gb/blog/changepower/201603/know-yourself-6-specific-ways-to-know-who-you-are?

Author photo © Nicola White @ Bunny and Blossom Photography

The moral rights of the author have been asserted.

All rights reserved. No part of this book may be reproduced by any mechanical, photographic or electronic process, or in the form of a phonographic recording; nor may it be stored in a retrieval system, transmitted or otherwise be copied for public or private use, other than for 'fair use' as brief quotations embodied in articles and reviews, without prior written permission of the publisher.

The information given in this book should not be treated as a substitute for professional medical advice; always consult a medical practitioner. Any use of information in this book is at the reader's discretion and risk. Neither the author nor the publisher can be held responsible for any loss, claim, or damage arising out of the use, or misuse, of the suggestions made, the failure to take medical advice, or for any material on third-party websites.

Case study names have been changed to maintain confidentiality.

A catalogue record for this book is available from the British Library.

Tradepaper ISBN: 978-1-83782-363-5
E-book ISBN: 978-1-83782-365-9
Audiobook ISBN: 978-1-83782-364-2

10 9 8 7 6 5 4 3 2 1

This product uses responsibly sourced papers, including recycled materials and materials from other controlled sources. For more information, see www.hayhouse.co.uk

The authorized representative in the EU for product safety and compliance is Penguin Random House Ireland, Morrison Chambers, 32 Nassau Street, Dublin D02 YH68, Ireland. https://eu-contact.penguin.ie

Printed and bound by CPI Group (UK) Ltd, Croydon CR0 4YY.

To my incredible husband, whose unwavering support and love guide me through every twist and turn of this life and my entrepreneurial journey: Your belief in me makes all things possible.

To Chelsey and Thea: May you always know that the world is wide open to your dreams and that, with courage and determination, anything is within your reach. Believe in yourself, and the possibilities are endless.

To my clients: You are my daily inspiration, reminding me of the power within each of us to transform, learn, and grow. Thank you for trusting me on your healing journey and with your dreams.

CONTENTS

Introduction — xi

Step 1: Amplify Your Awareness — 1

Step 2: Understand Your Narrative — 33

Step 3: Reject Old Stories — 65

Step 4: Become Your Authentic Self — 93

Step 5: Develop Your Self-Acceptance — 123

Step 6: Embrace Progression — 153

Step 7: Awaken the Higher Self — 181

My Final Note to You — 213
Further Reading — 217
Bonuses — 221
Thank Yous — 223
About the Author — 227

INTRODUCTION

On paper, people would have concluded that I was doing pretty well in life. However, despite the outward appearance of success, I was constantly battling comparison and self-doubt. I was chasing that elusive seven-figure mark in my business, but, subconsciously, I felt undeserving. I came to the uncomfortable realization that low self-esteem was still holding me back in my life and business. I'm sure many of you who have picked up this book can relate to that deep longing to fulfill your dreams, but you're being hindered by a voice inside that whispers, 'You're not good enough.' This shared struggle with self-doubt is what brings us together, and this book is all about finding the strength within to overcome these self-imposed limitations and achieve your true potential.

This book is for you if you're wrestling with self-doubt, yet, deep down, hold an unwavering desire for something greater than your current circumstances. You might feel destined for a life of mediocrity, but yearn to break free from low self-esteem and step into your higher power. Yet how can you embark on this transformative journey when you're unsure how or where to start? You're not alone; many underestimate their worth due to their low opinion of themselves. A recent study showed that one in five British women struggle with self-confidence, while a staggering 85 percent of their American counterparts suffer from low self-esteem.[1,2] So please don't feel alone – as the statistics indicate, you're certainly not the only one battling self-worth issues.

Over the past five years, I've shifted from a place of struggle and self-doubt to increased confidence, and new layers of healing from my own low self-esteem have taken place. This very book you're holding in your hands, or listening to, is a testament to that transformation. And I'm thrilled to be able to support you on your journey to overcoming low self-esteem. Before we get going, I want to share a little of my journey with you.

A LITTLE ABOUT ME

I felt like I'd been kicked in the stomach – that was how my partner at the time had just made me feel. In this moment, I can tell you I didn't feel enough. Looking back, it's one of the significant times in my life when I felt worthless, unloved, and lost. However, I still didn't leave the relationship after this incident. Then again, I hadn't left when I was cheated on or made to bear the burden of financial worry on my shoulders. So why would I leave now? I remained in this relationship despite knowing it wasn't healthy for me. 'Why?' you may ask. I'll tell you why: Because I believed that I was flawed and no one else could ever fall in love with me. Like so many of us who suffer from low self-esteem, I endured more disrespect and put up with behaviors that didn't align with my values. I chose to ignore my soul's calling, screaming for me to get out of this relationship. For you, it may not be about leaving a partner; it may be something

---

1   Ezadhyi, S. (2024), '1 in 5 Women Severely Lack Confidence, According to the UK's First Confidence Index', *Stylist* magazine, Sep: www.stylist.co.uk/health/mental-health/confidence-crisis-uk/940549 [Accessed July 30, 2025].

2   See Rubino, J. (2018), The Self-Esteem System™: theselfesteemsystem.com [Accessed July 30, 2025].

different, such as a toxic friendship, a job you hate, or an addiction. Whatever it is, staying in these situations reinforces day after day the perception that you're not enough. But this isn't true; we all have innate worth and value, and you deserve more. You're made for more!

Growing up in Nottingham, I struggled to find my place. Neither Black nor white, I never felt a sense of belonging, which was exacerbated by the bullying I endured throughout school. I also carried the weight of dyslexia, but without a diagnosis until much later in life, I received no support. Crippled by low self-esteem, I – like many other young people in my low-income area – developed a series of unhealthy relationships and turned to drinking, drugs, and shoplifting.

It took a long time for me to realize the impact that some of the experiences I encountered when younger had had on my self-esteem – particularly the effects of bullying and my racial heritage. People with low self-esteem often have high rates of self-criticism and tend to indulge in episodes of self-loathing. I know I certainly have over the years. So, it's no surprise that, if you suffer from low self-esteem, you're more likely to experience depression and have an increased risk of suicidal thoughts, eating disorders, and social anxiety. I'm open to sharing that depression is something I've battled with over the years, showing up as disordered eating patterns and suicidal thoughts. However, there was a turning point in my own experience of going through depression in my early twenties that led me to my first experience of attending counseling – it was only then that I started to make the connections between negative self-talk and low self-esteem. And, despite a difficult start in life, I always had an intuitive feeling that I was made for more. Although I wasn't always aligned with it, this inner guidance has been present from a young age.

This intuitive feeling has served as my guiding compass, helping me find my way through life, enabling me to see that my experiences aren't about me, but about how I can use them as a catalyst to support others. I knew that if I felt this way, many others likely felt the same. This led me to train as a psychotherapist and self-development coach.

As a seasoned psychotherapist, I have now supported hundreds of clients also grappling with low self-esteem. Many of them were unaware of the profound impact it was having on their lives until they began therapy with me. As a mixed-race, neurodivergent woman, I know how difficult it can be to access adequate support. My experience not only gives me a compassionate perspective with which to support the problematic journeys of others, but it informs my practice as a professional. I'm dedicated to being a vocal advocate for the marginalized, those who grew up like I did, for neurodivergent people, and also for practitioners working for future diversity within the profession.

Many of my clients come to therapy feeling unable to change how they view themselves, but my therapy initiatives provide the stepping stones to recovery and discovering their higher selves. My intention is always to make mental health support more accessible to the broadest range of people and give individuals who grew up the way I did a fighting chance of developing stronger mental resilience. This book serves as an extension of this desire – to reach beyond the one-to-one work I do, which is time-limited and relies on me being in the presence of the person I'm supporting, and to help you, the reader, too. I just knew this book had to be about adopting a more positive mindset and believing you're made for more, because without this core belief, we hold ourselves back in life.

BELIEVE YOU'RE MADE FOR MORE

One thing that has become clear to me from working with hundreds of clients in therapy is that when you feel flawed, you feel unworthy. Also, when you doubt that you're enough, you feel unlovable. This drastically alters your perception of what you deserve or can achieve. It can dictate every facet of your life – from jobs and relationships, to how you treat yourself. So many of my clients come to me with a hunger inside them – a deep desire to manifest their dreams – but this feels impossible for them to achieve because of their low self-worth. There are so many books, podcasts, and videos out there about manifesting and creating the life you desire, but, in my experience, until people truly understand their worth and have a strong belief in themselves, this simply leads to them striving for things in an unhealthy way, which ends up negatively impacting their mental health. Without strong self-esteem and self-belief, it's just not possible to manifest your dreams. Before your heart's desires can come to fruition, you must subconsciously and at a cellular level believe you're made for more.

I'm here to help you bridge that gap between low self-esteem and manifesting your dreams. Low self-esteem can be overcome – you don't have to accept that life will always feel this way. I believe everyone has the potential to live happily ever after. It begins with clearly declaring to the world that I AM WORTH IT! In *Believe You're Made for More*, I've drawn on years of experience, both personal and professional, to create a therapeutic framework specifically designed to help you shed old destructive thought patterns and to give you a unique opportunity to tap into your inner power and boost your self-esteem. This framework is enriched with examples from my extensive clientele and personal experiences to inspire you on your own journey and remind you that you're not alone.

I'm going to show you the steps to overcome low self-esteem, remember your worth, and develop quiet confidence. This quiet confidence is what I believe is necessary for you to transform your life. It's a feeling of inner trust and security that comes from within you. It's not gained from external forces or through the validation of others; it comes from the deeper relationship you have with yourself.

Being a therapist enables me to have a more nuanced and profound understanding of my clients' problems and, most importantly, the steps they can take to overcome them and reach what I term their 'higher self.' For me, the higher self is connected to my faith, which sustains in me an inner knowing and connection to the divine. In this book, I encourage you to seek out what you need to reach your true potential. *Believe You're Made for More* guides you through a transformation process, helping you to do just that.

While I've got you, it's essential to point out that this book is not a replacement for therapy; I always recommend that people seek professional support from a qualified mental health professional as and when they feel they need it.

HOW TO USE THIS BOOK

The first two steps in the book explore awareness of the issue at hand – low self-esteem – and the remaining steps are about how to build healthy self-esteem. For you to get the most out of the book, I believe the awareness parts are key to the start of your journey. So, I recommend that first-time readers work through the book from start to finish in a sequential order, as this will take you on a journey through the seven-step process. Once you've done this, you can then dip into each chapter as you see fit, or if there is a particular area you need to focus on. Each step is a process, with therapeutic exercises throughout. I recommend that you complete as many of

7 Steps to Your Higher Self

TRANSFORM – BELIEVE – ACHIEVE
More wealth, happiness, and abundance in your life

7. AWAKEN THE HIGHER SELF
The final step is to tap into your divine self – your nonmaterial dimension, soul, and spirit. This is the part of yourself that is unencumbered by ego.

6. EMBRACE PROGRESSION
Try new things that are good for you, welcome change, and evolve into the person you truly want to be.

5. DEVELOP YOUR SELF-ACCEPTANCE
Accept and be at peace with yourself, forgive yourself, and adopt a more compassionate relationship with the self.

4. BECOME YOUR AUTHENTIC SELF
Discover and understand who you are, your values, desires, and beliefs. This self-discovery forms the foundation for self-acceptance.

3. REJECT OLD STORIES
Let go of past narratives and create new, more balanced ways of seeing the world.

2. UNDERSTAND YOUR NARRATIVE
Explore your self-esteem story by asking yourself how your low self-esteem developed and has been maintained.

1. AMPLIFY YOUR AWARENESS
Notice how often you think negatively about yourself and consider the impact that these thoughts have on your life.

these exercises as you can to maximize the benefits of reading this book. Reflective practices can facilitate self-reflection, emotional processing, clarity, problem-solving, learning, stress reduction, and documenting personal growth. They are a powerful tool for self-discovery and raising self-esteem. While doing these exercises, feel free to write in the book and make it your own, or use a journal alongside it. You can also access your free downloadable *Believe You're Made for More* work booklet, in which you will find some of the exercises, at www.natashapagemsc.com.

I've included an affirmation at the end of each step, as well as a guided meditation. Affirmations can be powerful in reminding us of our potential and building a positive self-perception. You can use these affirmations in different ways – choose what feels best for you. Some ideas include simply taking note of these at the end of each chapter and repeating the affirmation in your head; or you can write them down on sticky notes and pop them where you'll see them regularly, such as on a bedroom mirror or bedside table. Alternatively, you can store them in your phone as reminders that pop up during the day, or you can record your own voice saying them and play them as a subliminal soundtrack – it can be very powerful to hear your own voice speak back affirmations to yourself.

When it comes to meditation, I used to struggle with the very idea of it, let alone the thought of practicing it daily. My neurodivergent brain usually means I flit from one thing to another and generally feel 'busy' in my mind. However, the introduction of meditation into my life has been a game changer. I used to think I couldn't meditate or do it properly, but I realized the trick is to find out how you can enjoy meditating. Some people like to meditate in silence, some with music, and others with guided meditation. I prefer the latter, and I specifically like to listen to recordings that also work on the subconscious mind. I now see meditation as an act of daily self-care and love, and I play audio meditations before sleep because I find this is a good time to incorporate them into my regular practice. I also encourage my clients to listen to meditations to help them on their journey and I urge you to do the same. You can listen to the meditations in each step in the audiobook and as a free audio journey on my website: www.natashapagemsc.com. I recommend that you use these audio versions if you can.

As we embark on this journey together, I'd also love to invite you to join my community of like-minded individuals on my website and follow me on Instagram @natashapagemsc – please do tag me with a copy of the book and say hello; I'd love to meet you.

I'm extremely excited and honored to work with you! Together, in this book, we'll embark on a personal and empowering journey – a journey that will change your life in so many beautiful ways.

Before we dive in, though, I want to just touch on the conditions we all need to thrive and grow…

FULFILL YOUR BASIC NEEDS FIRST

Before we can step into breaking free from the limited version of ourselves, it's essential to understand our basic needs first. Psychologist Abraham Maslow believed that to reach our full potential, we first need to have the necessities in place.[3] When people don't have the right conditions to thrive and grow, this can become an insurmountable problem, as I've seen demonstrated in my work as a therapist.

---

3   Maslow, A.H. (1954), *Motivation and Personality*. New York: Harper & Brothers.

Maslow's 'hierarchy of needs' is often presented as a five-tier pyramid:

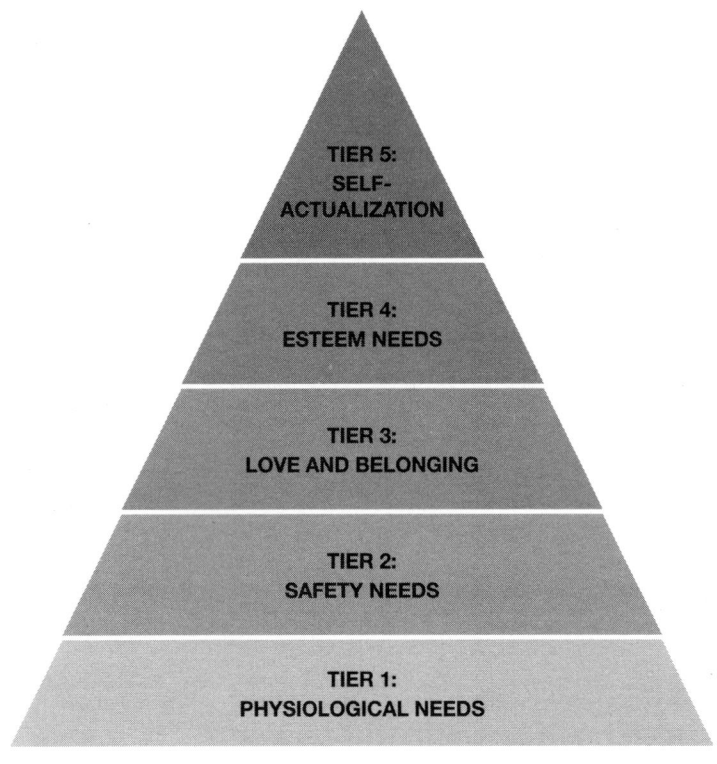

Maslow's 'hierarchy of needs' pyramid

Tier 1: Our physiological needs, which are the basic requirements for survival, such as food, water, shelter, and sleep.

Tier 2: Our safety needs – the security of our bodies, employment, resources, morality, health, and property.

Tier 3: The need for love and belonging, such as friendships, family, intimacy, and a sense of connection.

Tier 4: Our esteem needs – respect, self-esteem, status, recognition, strength, and freedom.

Tier 5: Self-actualization, which encompasses the desire to be the best that one can be. This part of the pyramid aligns us with the necessary conditions to step into our higher self. It's only once our esteem is in a good place that access to our higher self comes easily – life feels at ease, and you can reach your full potential. This is what we're working toward and will culminate in the final step in this book.

The bottom two levels (tiers 1 and 2) together make up basic needs, while self-actualization (tier 5) forms the tip of the pyramid. Needs lower down in the hierarchy must be satisfied before individuals' needs higher up can be addressed.

Maslow developed his theory during the Second World War, a time of global upheaval and change, when the world was grappling with immense loss, trauma, and transformation. This context influenced his emphasis on the individual's potential for growth, peace, and fulfillment beyond mere survival. Even though the majority of you reading this book are unlikely to be caught up in the awful atrocities of war, many of you may still lack the basic safety and security you need to thrive rather than simply survive. I've observed this in many clients who are stuck in unhealthy relationships and those who grapple with money struggles and poverty, and I know that some of these circumstances can feel beyond your control. However, I believe in the innate potential that all human beings have to make positive changes in their lives to thrive and grow into the person they want to be. As a therapist, I witness these transformations on a daily basis. So I urge you, whatever circumstances you're currently living in, never to lose sight of your ability as a human being to evolve, learn, and grow. As we'll see in Step 1, the challenges and difficulties we have in our lives are often a by-product of how we view ourselves, rather than the reality of the boundless potential we all hold within.

Take a few minutes to familiarize yourself with each level of Maslow's hierarchy of needs and reflect on what each means to you personally. Then complete our first exercise.

Reflecting on Your Needs

I would like you to think about your current life situation. What areas do you perceive as meeting your needs? Where do you feel there are gaps? Use these questions to guide your reflection.

Physiological Needs

- Do I have access to the basic necessities of life?
- Am I eating well and getting enough rest?
- In this area of my life, what am I grateful for?
- What would I like to change/improve in this area of my life?

Safety Needs

- Do I feel safe in my environment?
- Do I have financial stability and security?
- In this area of my life, what am I grateful for?
- What would I like to change/improve in this area of my life?

Love and Belonging

- Do I have meaningful relationships in my life?
- Do I feel a sense of connection and belonging?

- In this area of my life, what am I grateful for?
- What would I like to change/improve in this area of my life?

Esteem Needs

- Do I feel respected and valued?
- Do I have a sense of self-worth and confidence?
- In this area of my life, what am I grateful for?
- What would I like to change/improve in this area of my life?

Self-actualization

- Am I pursuing my passions and fulfilling my potential?
- Do I feel creative and fulfilled?
- In this area of my life, what am I grateful for?
- What would I like to change/improve in this area of my life?

Write down your thoughts and reflections on each level. Then consider the following prompts:

- Which needs are most pressing for me right now?
- Which needs are well met, and which ones require more attention?
- How do unmet needs affect my overall well-being?
- What steps can I take to better meet these needs?

Periodically, revisit this exercise to assess your progress and make adjustments as needed. Reflecting on your needs regularly can help you stay aware of your well-being and make proactive changes. By actively reading this book and working through the exercises, many people find that their needs are naturally met as they give more attention to these aspects of themselves.

....

Affirm:

I'm ready to step into my higher self and manifest all the things my heart desires. I'll do this one step at a time with love and patience on my journey.

AMPLIFY YOUR AWARENESS

Step 1

The first step is raising awareness of how low self-esteem impacts your life.

Welcome to the start of our journey together. In Step 1, we'll be raising your awareness of how low self-esteem impacts you, and exploring where you suffer from low self-esteem and how it affects your life, so that you can break free from the patterns that have been holding you hostage for too long. After all, how can we change our lives if we're completely unaware of how much these issues are affecting us?

WHAT IS SELF-ESTEEM?

As a therapist and coach, I see how self-esteem plays a crucial role in shaping our mental health and personal growth. It affects how we view ourselves, interact with others, and navigate life's challenges. But what do we actually mean by self-esteem?

Self-esteem is, in essence, the way we perceive and value ourselves – it's the core of how we navigate the world. It reflects our confidence in our abilities and how we view our worth. It influences our thoughts, feelings, and behaviors, our relationships with others and ourselves, our career choices, and beyond.

How we feel about ourselves can either aid our growth toward reaching our full potential – healthy self-esteem – or hold us back in a recurring cycle of self-doubt and fear – low self-esteem. People with healthy self-esteem recognize their strengths, accept their flaws, and feel comfortable with who they are. On the other hand, low self-esteem can manifest as self-doubt, feelings of inadequacy, and negative self-perception. I see this daily in my work with clients who struggle with self-doubt, and it can have a detrimental impact on their lives if it goes unresolved.

As a therapist, I encounter people with varying degrees of low self-esteem and it's important to note that self-esteem exists on a spectrum. Some people with low self-esteem find that it only affects them with certain people or situations and they battle only occasionally with negative self-talk. For others, it dominates every aspect of their experience and impacts everything they do, dramatically affecting their daily lives. Too little self-esteem can lead to constant self-criticism, while too much can lead to arrogance. Finding a healthy balance is key to emotional well-being.

Sigmund Freud's renowned work as a neurologist informed us that the brain functions with the id, ego, and superego; and these components play a huge role in shaping our self-esteem.[4] They influence how we perceive ourselves and how we respond to the world:

- **The id (instinctual desires):** The id operates on the pleasure principle, seeking instant gratification of desires and impulses. If the id heavily influences a person's self-esteem, they may base their self-worth on various forms of indulgence; for example, somebody who feels inadequate may indulge in shopping for items that make them feel good. This type of external validation is usually only temporary, leading to unstable or fleeting levels of confidence.

---

[4] Cornish, M. A. and Wade, N. G. (2015), 'A Therapeutic Model of Self-Forgiveness with Intervention Strategies for Counselors,' *Journal of Counseling and Development*, 93: 96–104: doi.org/10.1002/j.1556-6676.2015.00185.x [Accessed July 30, 2025].

- **The superego (moral standards):** The superego represents how we have internalized values from society, our parents, our peers, and so on. If we have a harsh, overactive superego, this can result in low self-esteem. This shows up in people who feel constant guilt and self-loathing, and find it hard to meet their own high standards. A healthy superego can help us foster self-worth.

- **The ego (balancing reality):** The ego mediates between the id and the superego, operating on the reality principle. A strong, well-balanced ego helps maintain healthy self-esteem, allowing a person to navigate desires and moral expectations realistically, fostering self-acceptance and resilience.

Self-esteem can be at risk if the id dominates, as it can lead to people needing external validation and being dependent on praise from others to keep them feeling OK about themselves. Equally, when the superego is overly critical or if the ego struggles to work through internal conflicts, self-esteem can be impacted. When someone can demonstrate self-compassion and confidence, the ego effectively integrates desires (the id) and values (the superego), leading to healthy self-esteem.

THE CONSEQUENCES OF LOW SELF-ESTEEM

Self-esteem is a cornerstone of mental and emotional health. It influences how we cope with life's challenges, our relationships, and what we view ourselves as capable of achieving. Low self-esteem can create barriers to growth and success, lead to us fearing failure and not wanting to get anything wrong, and prevent us from stepping out of our comfort zone. This can impact our quality of life and happiness.

People with low self-esteem might tolerate poor treatment or struggle with setting boundaries, because they don't believe they deserve better. Conversely, healthy self-esteem fosters resilience, encourages personal growth, and helps build more fulfilling relationships.

If you suffer from low self-esteem in some capacity, you might find yourself:

- using negative words or being critical toward yourself (for example, frequently telling yourself 'I'm not good enough' or 'I'll never succeed')
- using humor about yourself in a negative way
- focusing on the negative aspects of yourself and ignoring the positives
- blaming yourself when situations go wrong
- comparing yourself to others and feeling that others are superior to you
- feeling unworthy of pleasant things or having fun
- finding it hard to accept compliments
- avoiding new situations for fear of failing
- becoming disproportionately upset by criticism or people not approving of you
- often feeling low in mood, depressed, angry, ashamed, or worthless

Do any of these behaviors resonate with you? Even if you don't identify with all of them, it's helpful to be aware of them and mindful of these issues if they ever start to impact you, because – as we'll go on to explore in just a moment – the consequences of low self-esteem can be profound, hindering the realization of our true potential and our ability to live authentically.

Self-esteem is an emotion we innately feel inside, which is hard to express in words. Still, it impacts every aspect of our lived experience, including our relationships, happiness, and wealth. Like any aspect of our mental health, self-esteem can ebb and flow. It requires ongoing attention and care. Our experiences and interactions with others in life can influence it. But, ultimately, the higher our self-esteem, the less others can impact how we feel about ourselves.

Wherever you sit on the spectrum, it's vital to do inner work to heal from low self-esteem, because when you do, you start to develop a healthy relationship with yourself. You open your world to boundless possibilities. Life changes and takes on new meaning. You can step into your higher power when you fully embrace who you are. I've seen this so often in my own life and with those I work with. Now it's your time, too.

Before we dive deeper into how low self-esteem might be impacting you, I would like you to take a questionnaire widely used by therapists worldwide to evaluate individual self-esteem. All credit goes to Morris Rosenberg, who has kindly permitted clinicians to use his questionnaire free of charge if we cite his work. This is from his book *Conceiving the Self*.[5]

---

5 Rosenberg, M. (1979), *Conceiving the Self*. New York: Basic Books.

Self-Esteem Questionnaire

This questionnaire is a valuable tool designed to help you gain insights into your own self-perception and confidence levels. By completing this exercise, you take an important first step toward self-awareness and personal growth.

Here is a list of statements dealing with your general feelings about yourself. Please indicate how strongly you agree or disagree with each statement by circling 'Strongly Agree,' 'Agree,' 'Disagree,' or 'Strongly Disagree.' The online version of this questionnaire is available on my website: www.natashapagemsc.com.

1. On the whole, I am satisfied with myself.

Strongly Agree ❏ Agree ❏ Disagree ❏ Strongly Disagree ❏

2. At times, I think I am no good at all.

Strongly Agree ❏ Agree ❏ Disagree ❏ Strongly Disagree ❏

3. I feel that I have a number of good qualities.

Strongly Agree ❏ Agree ❏ Disagree ❏ Strongly Disagree ❏

4. I am able to do things as well as most other people.

Strongly Agree ❏ Agree ❏ Disagree ❏ Strongly Disagree ❏

5. I feel I do not have much to be proud of.

Strongly Agree ❏ Agree ❏ Disagree ❏ Strongly Disagree ❏

6. I certainly feel useless at times.

Strongly Agree ❏ Agree ❏ Disagree ❏ Strongly Disagree ❏

7. I feel that I'm a person of worth, at least on an equal plane with others.

Strongly Agree ❏ Agree ❏ Disagree ❏ Strongly Disagree ❏

8. I wish I could have more respect for myself.

Strongly Agree ❑ Agree ❑ Disagree ❑ Strongly Disagree ❑

9. All in all, I am inclined to feel that I am a failure.

Strongly Agree ❑ Agree ❑ Disagree ❑ Strongly Disagree ❑

10. I take a positive attitude toward myself.

Strongly Agree ❑ Agree ❑ Disagree ❑ Strongly Disagree ❑

When you have answered all the questions, use this key to tally up your score and obtain the total:

For the statements 1, 3, 4, 7, and 10, the points are scored one way:

Strongly Agree = 3 points

Agree = 2 points

Disagree = 1 points

Strongly Disagree = 0 points

For the statements 2, 5, 6, 8, and 9, the points are scored in reverse:

Strongly Agree = 0 points

Agree = 1 points

Disagree = 2 points

Strongly Disagree = 3 points

The scale ranges from 0 to 30, with higher scores corresponding to greater levels of self-esteem.

....

It's helpful to remember that self-esteem isn't fixed; it can fluctuate according to various factors, such as experiences, relationships, and self-perception. Therefore, regardless of your score on the questionnaire, self-reflection and evaluation can be incredibly beneficial. Even if you receive a low score, it's important to view this information as an opportunity to understand yourself and your starting base level.

Remember that self-esteem is a journey; every step you take toward self-awareness and self-acceptance is meaningful.

Doing this questionnaire is an essential starting point. Regardless of the outcome, it demonstrates a commitment to reflection and personal growth. Let's celebrate that!

Are you surprised by your score? Yes or no? Sometimes we may have a different perception of ourselves than the questionnaire reveals. This is OK. Whether the score was higher or lower, your feelings are valid. Remember, this is just a snapshot of where you are right now. The value of this questionnaire is that it highlights the areas of strength and areas for growth. The score doesn't define you; it's a tool that helps you start the journey toward building greater self-esteem and confidence – and becoming the version of yourself that you aspire to be.

THE IMPACT OF LOW SELF-ESTEEM

As we've seen, low self-esteem goes beyond feelings of occasional self-doubt. It erodes our sense of self, and it consistently means we doubt our worth and abilities and the value we contribute to the world. It's often present in the inner whispers of our minds. My clients come to see me with so many varied things that affect their self-esteem – from race, childhood experiences, and bullying, to cosmetic procedures such as breast reductions or enlargements that have really affected how they feel about themselves.

Many of us are unaware of the impact of low self-esteem on our lives, as it often manifests in very subtle yet profound ways. As a therapist, I witness this struggle daily, often unnoticed by those within its grasp. Unbeknown to many, low self-esteem leads to a vicious circle that quietly robs them of life's rich experiences – and this lack of experiences then leads to further low self-esteem. This is why the first step focuses on amplifying your awareness to help you become attuned to the avoidance behaviors and coping mechanisms that keep the cycle of low self-esteem going. This will help you develop strategies for dealing with intrusive thoughts, understand how you can counterbalance your thoughts, and, in turn, give you more control to change these patterns into healthier ways of being.

On Our Relationships

Do you ever feel like you're not good enough in your relationships? In my role supporting others, I often see how those with low self-esteem can create an internal hidden barrier that sabotages their ability to connect and enjoy authentic and enriching relationships – whether it's in their role as a parent, partner, or friend.

Low self-esteem can have a detrimental impact on our relationships, making us feel undeserving of love, respect, or kindness. In our romantic relationships, it can lead to us pushing people away as we fear rejection, or clinging tightly to a relationship for fear that the other person will leave. I frequently see how people settle for less when a relationship is unhealthy; they let the relationship continue even though they don't feel loved, valued, or respected.

Low self-esteem can also manifest in other ways, such as an unfulfilling sex life where you don't express your needs and desires and settle for less in all areas of the relationship; or you may tolerate toxic or abusive behaviors and have a deep-seated belief that the other person will leave you, because you don't feel good enough – as you saw in the Introduction, I myself fell into this trap. It can also manifest as jealousy, comparing yourself to others, or insecurity.

Siobhan's Story

Siobhan, 35, went through a relationship breakdown. She had been in the relationship for 10 years and had deeply wanted the relationship to progress into marriage, and to have children. She didn't ever bring this up with her partner, because she knew he didn't share the same view as her. She was worried she wouldn't find another relationship, because, deep down, she didn't feel lovable and doubted that anyone would want to commit to a relationship with her. So, she remained in the relationship while secretly keeping her wishes and needs to herself. Unfortunately, despite this, her partner decided he wanted to move to Australia and didn't wish to remain in the relationship. The separation left her grappling with profound insecurities about her ability to find love again. Her low self-esteem and the fear that no one would ever find her attractive drove her into a negative cycle of engaging in unhealthy relationships.

In response to her fear, she found herself repeatedly falling into unsupportive relationship patterns, seeking validation and security from partners who weren't respectful of her and who just wanted to have sex without any commitments. At first, this seemed OK for her, but after a few encounters, she realized that this further impacted her low self-esteem, as she wasn't gaining what she wanted from the relationships.

Once she started to identify the links between her negative relationship patterns and the fears that drove her to act out in this way, her coping mechanisms and avoidance behaviors (which, for her, was about avoiding being single) started to become clear to her. This enabled her to move forward and commit to developing a healthier perception of herself, rebuilding her self-esteem and self-worth outside of a romantic relationship. She started taking part in activities she enjoyed, such as going to the gym, crafting, and joining a reading club. Through the more profound love she found for herself, she established and maintained healthy boundaries in her pursuit of a relationship. With her new-found self-awareness and confidence, she approached dating with a healthier mindset, prioritizing her well-being and choosing partners who aligned with her values and goals. While her healing journey wasn't without its challenges, she emerged more robust and resilient, ready to embrace the possibility of love and genuine connection again.

We'll be exploring which avoidance behaviors and coping mechanisms you might be adopting in just a bit, so that you too can gain awareness and break free of them.

Low self-esteem can affect relationships across the board – not only in our romantic relationships, but also with our friends and family. It's incredibly difficult to forge real, genuine connections with others when we're shrouded by our own insecurities.

I see how often people with low self-esteem put the needs of others first. Their fear of not being good enough in their friendships leads to overcompensating in their relationships. This shows up as conflict avoidance, struggles to maintain boundaries or assert their needs and opinions, and a tendency to over-give. This can lead to burnout or resentment in what can feel like non-reciprocal friendships. The fear of rejection makes it highly challenging for these people to open up fully and be their authentic selves, and this prevents them from truly connecting with others.

On Our Work, Career, or in Business

Low self-esteem can impact your professional relationships. It may hinder your ability to communicate effectively in workplace settings, affect how you interact with others, or prevent you from advocating for yourself. Low self-esteem also stops you from expressing your ideas and voicing your opinions – you second-guess your contributions and defer to others. It makes you avoid challenges or underestimate your abilities, and keeps you from progressing in your career or from applying for a promotion for fear that you'll be unsuccessful. You may avoid leadership roles even when you're qualified for them. This can lead to role stagnation, missed opportunities, and not pursuing the chance to evolve and grow.

Low self-esteem in the workplace also manifests in us overworking, trying to prove our worth or making sure everything we do is perfect. This can present itself as hypersensitivity, making us perceive constructive feedback as criticism, and leading to strained relationships with our peers and supervisors at work. Similar to our other relationships, we seek external validation from colleagues or managers. When positive feedback isn't received, this can lead to feelings of insecurity. When our worth is reliant on the opinions of others, the pressure to please everyone becomes stressful and can lead to burnout, which impacts our emotional well-being.

Low self-esteem can stop us from pursuing the goal of running our own businesses, as we fear failure so much that we avoid new projects or challenges. Low self-esteem robs us of our dreams, limits us, puts us in a box, and stops us from realizing our professional potential.

On Our Mental Health

Our self-esteem is linked closely to our mental health and well-being. When our self-esteem is low, we have more chance of developing mental health conditions such as anxiety and depression. The negative internal dialogue that plays on autopilot when we have low self-esteem leads some of us to experience feelings of hopelessness.

On Our Personal Goals

Low self-esteem can diminish the pursuit of our dreams and prevent us from working toward what we want to achieve in life. It can hold us back, stopping us from taking risks, reaching our fullest potential, and living from our highest selves.

••••

As you can see, low self-esteem can be a silent yet constant presence in the background of our lives. It makes us isolate ourselves and shrink away when we would benefit from the opposite – connection and support from others. It can also lead to unhealthy coping mechanisms and avoidance behaviors, which can cause low mood, depression, and anxiety. Let's explore these now.

COMMON AVOIDANCE BEHAVIORS AND COPING MECHANISMS

We'll now explore some common avoidance behaviors and unhealthy coping mechanisms that keep the cycle of low self-esteem going.

Knowing about these is essential, because they can be subtle and often go unnoticed, as people who have become accustomed to low self-esteem often engage in them automatically. See if you identify with any of the following descriptions. Remember, with awareness, you can then develop strategies to change these patterns.

Social Withdrawal

Avoidance behavior: You withdraw from social interactions to reduce the risk of potential criticism or rejection.

Coping mechanism: Social withdrawal provides immediate relief from the fear of negative judgment, but reinforces isolation, limiting opportunities for positive social interactions.

Social withdrawal leads to you avoiding situations or experiences that make you feel socially challenged. You often feel hindered from embracing social opportunities and seeing them as positive experiences. This is the ego seeking to keep you safe from encounters you view as dangerous in order to avoid the risk of criticism or rejection. The sad thing about withdrawal is that it stops you from living life to the full and doesn't allow you to develop your capabilities or learn and grow.

People socially withdraw in many different and creative ways. Perhaps you're quick to decline invitations, or you cancel your plans at the last minute for the most random of excuses. Avoiding parties or other social gatherings is a common scenario. However, withdrawal can also manifest in normal day-to-day activities. One of my clients once explained the difficulty of asking colleagues if they wanted a cup of tea. This made the client feel anxious and awkward. Intrusive thoughts would enter their mind, and they started to worry about getting things wrong. They experienced thoughts such as: 'What if I don't make their tea to their liking?,' 'If I ask them if they want tea, should I ask everybody in the room too?,' and 'What will they think of me?' What may seem like a simple task for many created a tremendous amount of anxiety for this client, so they avoided asking people if they wanted a hot drink.

Social withdrawal affects people in various ways. Perhaps you struggle to express your thoughts and opinions in a work meeting or share your true feelings with family and friends. Deep within your heart is a longing to voice your new idea and share your excitement, but the fear of being rejected or mocked in some way weighs heavily on your mind and keeps you from expressing yourself. Low self-esteem leads to you retreating and not sharing your opinions, thoughts, and ideas. Sadly, the world misses out on these valuable contributions. People don't have full access to you and may not be able to engage fully with you at a deeper level, which is sad. When we have high self-esteem, we know everyone's opinion is essential and we allow ourselves to have differing views. We may sometimes get things wrong and even say stupid things, and we can cope with this. But low self-esteem makes this feel way too scary – we can't risk the embarrassment.

Another belief that many of you may hold is that no one is interested in hearing what you have to say, because you're unnecessary and your views don't matter. This can lead to many missed opportunities in life, especially regarding relationships, as you don't share your genuine opinions.

Low self-esteem can also impact your ability to assert yourself in situations you don't feel happy with. You tend to go with the flow and accept things you don't want for fear of being judged or causing conflict.

You may also be more prone to using alcohol or other forms of recreational drugs to help you mask your anxiety in social settings. Alcohol can be used as a way to help you feel more relaxed and lose your inhibitions, but this only serves as a temporary relief from the complicated emotions and experiences associated with low self-esteem.

This book will help you to develop new ways of managing difficult emotions and enable you to adopt healthier ways of viewing those situations that may once have challenged you.

Perfectionism

Avoidance behavior: You set unrealistic standards to live by to avoid failure and being criticized.

Coping mechanism: To alleviate feelings of inadequacy, you strive for perfection, but in pursuing perfection, you burn yourself out emotionally and physically. While this may provide temporary relief from feelings of inadequacy, it can also increase anxiety and distort your sense of self in the long term.

You just won't take anything less than perfect, you push yourself hard, and you strive to get the best results you can. It doesn't matter if you're working late, neglecting your needs, or feeling stressed to the max, you will keep on pushing through, because you won't stop at anything less than perfect! Does this sound familiar? The thing is, perfectionism is used to avoid failure and criticism.

By setting unrealistic targets and adhering to excessively high standards, people often end up working harder than necessary. I see this manifest for my clients in scenarios such as the workplace. These are the people-pleasers who take on tasks even when they're stretched. They don't say no. They will take jobs home, work beyond their contractual hours, and strive to the best of their ability. They often appear to be high achievers who seem to have everything under control. However, internally they're struggling, frequently experiencing episodes of stress and anxiety from the immense pressure they place on themselves. In relationships and friendships alike, they will go above and beyond, desperately seeking to keep others happy, including through excessive acts of service, buying gifts, or conforming to things they don't feel aligned with. They never want to show signs of being less than perfect, because this brings up fears of rejection. It gives rise to jealousy and insecurities in their relationships, as they question their worthiness of their friends' or partner's love.

If you recognize yourself in this description, the steps in this book will help you become more aware of when you may be doing this and suggest strategies you can use to break free break free from this type of behavior.

Self-Deprecation

Avoidance behavior: You find yourself talking negatively to yourself and ruminating on self-critical thoughts.

Coping mechanism: Self-deprecation acts as a defense mechanism against external criticism, but it strengthens the negative cycle of low self-esteem as you reinforce your negative perception of yourself.

Are you the first person to declare how bad your hair looks or how much weight you've put on? Maybe you throw casual insults at yourself about your lack of capabilities. This is your inner critic at play, pointing out your flaws, criticizing your actions, and generally impacting your self-worth – it's a common thread among those who suffer from low self-esteem.

You might also use humor to make yourself feel safe, because it gives you a sense of control over other people who are checking you out or pointing out your flaws. It feels much safer to take control of what others may think of you than to leave this to chance, so you enter a cycle of self-perpetuating abuse, because this feels way less harmful than leaving it in the hands of others. But each negative jibe you direct toward yourself reinforces the belief that you aren't good enough. You may use self-deprecation as a coping mechanism to lessen the impact of external criticism. Still, it exacerbates your negative self-perception and, as a result, contributes to the maintenance of low self-esteem.

In therapy, I assist my clients by teaching them to observe and politely silence their inner critic. It's important to know that this inner critic (our ego) is just that – a critic – and what it says isn't necessarily true or a fact. We'll be doing some work together on silencing your own inner critic as we progress through the steps.

Procrastination

Avoidance behavior: You postpone tasks or avoid challenges to prevent potential failure.

Coping mechanism: Procrastination provides temporary relief from facing your perceived threats. However, this often results in increased stress, missed opportunities, and a reinforcing cycle of self-doubt. Avoiding challenges provides a sense of safety in the short term, but hinders personal growth and reinforces the belief that you're incapable or unworthy.

Do you find yourself putting off tasks that you know you need to complete? Do you know, deep inside, that doing that thing will help you progress or feel more organized, but you stall and stall and stall? Procrastination is often associated with being lazy or mismanaging your time. However, it's also one of the many sophisticated ways we manage our low self-esteem. There's some clever neuroscience behind this…

Research studies have concluded that self-esteem has been shown to be a critical predictor of general procrastination, with lower self-esteem individuals exhibiting higher procrastination levels.[6] The ego part of the brain that we met earlier does its utmost to protect us from scenarios that may hurt or harm us. It's constantly searching for any situation's potential rewards and risks. When we have low self-esteem and encounter new situations, these can be difficult to adjust to. They can activate our internal alarm system, making us perceive the situation as a threat. As wonderful as they are, our brains don't distinguish between real life-threatening situations and experiences that are taking us out of our comfort zone. So, it feels safest to delay the action. This may not even be a conscious decision – it can be a subconscious, automatic reaction, which is why it's essential to become aware of when you might be doing this. The steps in this book will help you to become more attuned to the subtle ways you avoid taking action and will help you to reduce or stop these behaviors.

When you have healthy self-esteem, you trust in yourself and have an innate knowing that you can succeed at things. You're more optimistic and capable of undertaking tasks you haven't done before, with the confidence that you will succeed – but you also accept the risk of failure. When you have low self-esteem, you don't have confidence in yourself or believe you'll succeed. This means a lack of motivation sets in, because you don't see pursuing the task as

---

6   Ferrari, J. R. (2000), 'Procrastination and Attention: Factor Analysis of Attention Deficit, Boredomness, Intelligence, Self-Esteem, and Task Delay Frequencies,' *Journal of Social Behavior & Personality*, 15: 185–96.

having any benefit or reward. Intuitively, it makes sense. Why would you invest your time and energy in a task when you feel destined to fail? This negative-thinking cycle can prevent you from completing even those projects that you may feel more confident about, as your low self-esteem makes you doubt your ability to achieve them. This often stems from procrastination itself, therefore creating a negative cycle.

Putting Up Emotional Defenses

Avoidance behavior: You may repress, deny, or project your feelings to protect yourself from uncomfortable emotions.

Coping mechanism: Emotional defenses are unconscious psychological strategies that help us to manage stress, anxiety, and emotional distress. While they can be helpful in the moment, they can also stop you developing self-awareness.

For example, do you find yourself saying that something is OK when, really, deep inside, you feel sad or angry? This is one instance of an emotional defense, where you suppress your true feelings out of fear of a negative outcome, such as conflict or rejection from others. Instead of expressing your feelings healthily, you suppress them because to do otherwise feels unsafe.

Working through the steps in this book will help you become more attuned to your needs and emotions – and therefore less likely to feel the need to suppress them, making you more able to approach situations in an effective way.

Exploring Your Avoidance Behaviors

I'd like you to take some time to reflect on the different areas of your life where avoidance behaviors may be affecting you. This can help you break free from avoidance and the negative cycles that could be holding you back.

1. Look at the different areas of life often impacted by avoidance behaviors:

    - work
    - relationships
    - self-care
    - personal goals

    For each of these areas, write down how avoidance has impacted you in the past or impacts you now. This can relate to specific tasks, scenarios, or emotions you avoid. In particular, consider those moments when you feel anxious, procrastinate, or make excuses. For example, you might write: 'At work, I don't contribute my opinions and ideas in meetings in case people think my ideas are stupid.'

2. Now, let's explore the roots behind the avoidance. For each area you've identified, reflect on the following questions:

    - What thoughts or feelings arise when I think about facing this task or situation?
    - Am I afraid of failure, rejection, discomfort, or something else?
    - What beliefs or past experiences might be contributing to this avoidance?

    Write down your reflections, being as honest and detailed as possible.

3. Then, consider the impact of avoidance. Imagine what your life might look like if you stopped avoiding and started facing these situations head-on. How could this positively impact your life? How might you feel about yourself? Write in as much detail as you can how this would look and feel.

....

SHORT-TERM RELIEF = LONG-TERM IMPACT

We've explored how you might use avoidance behaviors and coping mechanisms to gain short-term relief from uncomfortable thoughts or feelings about yourself. Indeed, they serve an excellent purpose in shielding us from threats to our self-esteem. However, the long-term impact of these is detrimental, because we can become trapped in a negative feedback loop that reinforces our inability to step up to challenges in life.

Social withdrawal can lead to increased isolation and reduce the positive social interactions you can access. You can get stuck in unhelpful behavior patterns that can hinder your development of healthy relationships. Perfectionism and self-deprecation can result in crippling anxiety and a distorted image of yourself, which further impacts your self-esteem. Procrastination and avoidance limit your growth and keep you stuck in a negative cycle where life doesn't change or improve, further reinforcing feelings of self-loathing. And putting up emotional defenses can mean you become detached from your real emotions, which then affects the quality of your relationships, as well as your mental health.

Recognizing and addressing low self-esteem allows you to reclaim your worth and live a more fulfilling life. I've experienced first-hand how damaging low self-esteem can be, but I've also seen how working on it can lead to profound change.

HOW SOCIAL MESSAGES IMPACT SELF-ESTEEM

The avoidance behaviors and coping mechanisms we've just explored all come from *inside* you – your own perceptions – but there are also some external influences that can impact your self-esteem.

Without being aware of it, we often internalize cultural norms, values, and beliefs through socialization – what I term social messages. We constantly pick up on the social messages fed to our unconscious minds. Some examples include: 'Men are strong and women are nurturing'; 'I must work hard to make money'; or 'I have to be slim to be beautiful'… the list is endless. We're all prone to buying into these social messages to a degree. However, we must be especially aware of this when we suffer from low self-esteem, because then we become even more susceptible to taking them on. This is because low self-esteem makes us very conscious of what others think or expect from us, so we try to conform. I know I've certainly taken on social messages over my lifetime.

For example, I grew up in a blended cultural household with many different music genres and developed a very eclectic taste. As a younger child, I danced around the living room to music by Tina Turner, David Bowie, Elvis, and Earth, Wind & Fire. I wasn't aware of the ethnicity of the artists or genre; I just liked the music. In my teenage years, I became more conscious of what music I listened to and what others in my peer group might think of me. I had a genuine love of listening to music of Black origin – R&B and rap music – but I also felt an expectation that this was the music I *should* be listening to because of my Black heritage. I felt like I had to conform and fit in with other people's perceptions of what a Black teenager should listen to. It wasn't until my later teens that I could embrace the fact that I liked all kinds of music and that this was OK.

The thing about low self-esteem is that you don't want to deviate from the norm, and so you lose a sense of your own identity. Adolescence is a unique period in which we try to figure out who we are. However, low self-esteem can continue into adulthood, and this can stop us from expressing who we really are. We don't develop a strong identity or confidence in sharing our preferences, life choices, clothing style, or music. At worst, we may lose a sense of ourselves and not even fully know what we like or dislike.

Perceptions of Beauty

One of the things I've battled with as a mixed-race woman is the notion of not feeling like I fitted into social perceptions of beauty. Firstly, the general issue of where I fitted was something I battled with as a teen, knowing that part of society viewed me as a Black woman while others viewed me as someone who was mixed-race. Although I don't find it offensive when someone calls me a Black woman, I believe that this term fails to acknowledge the dual parts of my heritage. However, these initial identity crises can impact our development of a strong sense of self.

During the eighties and nineties, the era in which I grew up, women like Pamela Anderson, Kylie Minogue, and Madonna were iconic figures. The social messages that fed into those years were that you had to be petite, white, blonde, blue-eyed, and have big breasts to qualify as attractive in society. So it's no wonder these were the messages I started taking on. As a tall, curvy, mixed-race brunette, I didn't fit into those cultural perceptions of beauty. And when you don't see yourself fitting into these narrow social beauty ideals, you don't like what you see in the mirror. I see this often as a therapist. It can lead to people developing a negative relationship with themselves. They can also start to feel envious of others they deem more attractive and may feel like they aren't good enough.

What social messages feed into creating and maintaining your low self-esteem? Are you aware of them? In the following exercise, I want you to realize how many social messages have found their way into your head and how they make you feel.

Evaluating Social Messages

Take a few moments to pause and reflect on these questions:

1. What does society tell you about success, beauty, gender, and so on?

2. How do you measure your own worth based on others' perceived successes or failures – for example, through social media comparisons?

3. How do your answers to these questions make you feel about yourself?

Congratulations – you've worked through Step 1 and are now well on your way to amplifying your awareness of how low self-esteem might be manifesting in everything from your mental health to your relationships and personal growth. We've exposed the many sophisticated avoidance behaviors and coping strategies you might be implementing to manage your low self-esteem and how they can keep your negative self-perception going. I hope you feel empowered now that you're armed with this knowledge.

We'll now move on to practice some further therapeutic exercises that will help consolidate your learning. Each exercise is designed to heighten your awareness of the impact of low self-esteem on your life. Those of us with low self-esteem need to recognize how self-esteem affects us first, before we can seek support and gradually replace maladaptive coping mechanisms with healthier strategies to foster long-term improvement.

THERAPEUTIC EXERCISES

Creating a Self-Esteem Inventory

For this exercise, I would like you to create a self-esteem inventory. This will help you to identify areas where you feel confident and good about yourself, as well as those where you feel insecure. Completing this exercise will also help you identify patterns and triggers related to your self-esteem. For example:

Areas I feel confident in are: I'm a good cook, I'm caring, and I'm organized.

Areas I feel insecure about are: my level of education, my appearance, and my ability to hold a conversation.

Now it's your turn.

Shifting Perspective

For this exercise, you will need a quiet space to connect with and tune in to your inner thoughts and reflections.

1. First, I'd like you to write down a description of yourself from the perspective of low self-esteem. These are the thoughts that are present in your low moments.

2. Now, I'd like you to do the same from a place of good self-esteem, in the knowledge that this doesn't mean pretending you're perfect (no one is perfect). What would you say to yourself if you were your own best friend?

3. To help you reflect on your perception of self-worth, please answer the following questions:

    - When do you feel the most insecure?
    - What negative thoughts do you feel people have about you?
    - When do you not feel enough?
    - When do you feel a higher sense of worth?

Now that you have a clearer understanding, you can start taking action to improve your self-esteem. In the steps that follow, we'll be looking at how you can recognize and challenge negative thoughts; set realistic goals and celebrate small achievements; build a support network of positive and understanding individuals; and engage in activities that promote self-compassion and self-care – all of which will help you to transform your self-esteem. You may also find it helpful to seek professional support through therapy or counseling.

Amplifying Your Awareness Guided Meditation

1. Make yourself comfortable. Close your eyes if this feels comfortable for you and focus on your breath. As you focus on your breath, breathe deeply and slowly. Stay like this for a few moments until you enter a deep state of relaxation.

2. Take a moment to identify one or two ways in which low self-esteem has held you back: How has it interfered with your life? It may have caused doubt, fear, self-loathing, or criticism. It may have made you feel like you're 'not good enough' or 'like a failure,' or stopped you from pursuing your goals and dreams in life.

3. Let go of judgment around this and simply acknowledge its presence.

4. Notice how these thoughts make you feel. How do they affect your body? Do they make you feel tense and anxious? Do you feel a sense of burden and stress? Where do you feel this in your body? Simply acknowledge the feeling without trying to change anything just yet. Allow yourself to feel the full impact that these thoughts have on you. Amplifying your awareness is the key to letting go and stepping into your true power.

5. With each breath you take, realize that you're creating more space between yourself and your low self-esteem. Start visualizing it as being separate from who you really are. Realize that you are not your doubts or fears; you're simply an observer. Amplifying your awareness of how this has held you back is critical to letting it go.

6. Now that you've let go of low self-esteem, it's time to introduce a new, more positive outlook on yourself. Consider the way you have been viewing yourself. What might be a more balanced and loving way to view who you

are? For example, if you don't feel good enough, replace that feeling with 'I am enough just as I am.' Take a moment to find a positive affirmation that resonates with you.

7. Now repeat this affirmation silently to yourself or out loud. Notice how it feels in your body. Does it bring a sense of peace, happiness, and warmth within? Feel this truth resonate with your inner self, dissolving any of the old thoughts you once had.

8. Now, imagine you're living a life aligned to the new belief you hold about yourself. See how you move through your days with inner confidence, self-love, and compassion. Notice how you approach challenges in your life and how you care for yourself. This is you – and you're strong, capable, and worthy of all good things. Spend a few moments reflecting on this vision.

9. To close, repeat to yourself, 'I am aware of my low self-esteem, but I reject this version of me and choose to embrace who I am. I replace low self-esteem with self-love and compassion.' Take a few deep breaths, and embrace this affirmation in your heart.

10. When you feel ready, slowly bring your awareness back to the present moment and open your eyes if they were closed.

11. Carry this sense of positivity and self-awareness with you as you move through your day. Remember, you have the power to amplify your awareness. Select the way you view yourself and choose to treat yourself with love and kindness.

....

Affirm:

I reject the old coping strategies that didn't serve me, and I adopt a healthy attitude by loving myself as I am and for who I am.

UNDERSTAND YOUR NARRATIVE

Step 2

The second step is understanding how your low self-esteem developed and how that narrative is maintained.

Now that you have amplified your awareness of how low self-esteem might be impacting your daily life, this step is all about diving deeper and looking at the stories you tell yourself – your narrative – that contribute to low self-esteem.

Your narrative may be based on the stories others have created or the ones you have told yourself over time – the stories you play out in your conscious and subconscious mind. Understanding your narrative is crucial to deepening your self-perception and recognizing how it impacts your self-esteem and overall relationship with yourself. It's key to building more positive self-esteem now and in the future. When we recognize how our narrative has shaped who we are and what we believe, this helps us understand why we feel the way we do about ourselves.

I assist many of my clients by exploring their past, which helps them gain more clarity about their feelings in the present. This enables them to unearth the roots of their low self-esteem, which is another step toward fostering positive change. Often, we're unaware of how much our narrative impacts our lives, so let's spend some time now exploring your self-esteem story.

WHAT IS YOUR NARRATIVE?

Understanding the narrative you tell yourself is important, because it forms the foundation of how you view yourself, what you believe you can achieve, and, ultimately, what you think you're worth. It's a perspective on the world around you, and how you interpret things through your eyes. Through a deeper understanding of this narrative, you can ensure you aren't limiting yourself, seeing yourself through a negative lens, or hindering the joy you could experience in life.

People with low self-esteem hold a negative perception of themselves; they live with a limiting story often created during their early life experiences and then continuing throughout their lifespan. In my work as a therapist, people share these deep-rooted negative perceptions of themselves with me all the time. Clients tell me they have thoughts such as 'I'm not attractive enough,' 'I'm not intelligent,' 'I'm not capable,' 'I won't ever achieve what I want to,' 'I'll never earn as much as I want to,' 'My family don't achieve things,' 'I'm not good enough,' 'I let people down,' or 'I'm too fat/skinny/tall/short.'

The narrative we tell ourselves is the very essence of who we become. The route to creating a happier, more fulfilled, and abundant life is to reject the narrative you once told yourself – the stories that make you believe you aren't enough – and to start creating a new narrative, a new way of seeing yourself.

> ### Martin's Story
>
> Martin, 24, shared how his parents always compared him to his older brother, who he felt his parents saw as the golden child. He told me: 'He achieved straight As and was signed to a football club as a teenager. I was just average. I wasn't academic and I wasn't good at

football either. I began to believe that I was only worth something if I could match up to him. But I never could.'

This narrative – that he wasn't good enough – followed Martin into adulthood. As an adult, he sought validation in every corner of his life, trying to compensate for his low self-esteem. He worked long hours, often taking on more than he could handle, believing that if he could achieve more and prove his worth to others, he would finally feel good enough.

When I worked with Martin, I helped him to understand how this made him feel as a child. We explored a child's perceptions and that children are more likely to misinterpret situations. I challenged Martin to explore other untrue things he may have believed as a child. He agreed that some of them weren't factual. This helped him start rewriting the narrative he'd told himself for so long and to realize that, just because he didn't have the same traits as his brother, this didn't mean he wasn't good enough.

Experiences like Martin's are very common. From an early age, we start to build our narrative on how we experience and perceive the world and the way we interpret these events. For Martin, he felt his parents held his brother in higher esteem and he interpreted this as meaning he wasn't good enough. For others, it might be that they aren't as pretty as others, they aren't clever, or they aren't lovable. Do you tell yourself stories like these? Do you cling to past experiences that made you feel you weren't good enough? You'll get a chance to explore this further in the exercise on pages 51–54, but, first, let's look at some of the factors that shape our narratives.

WHERE DO THESE NARRATIVES COME FROM?

We're now going to explore some of the common influences and experiences that shape the stories we tell ourselves in more depth. It can be helpful to make these connections and reflect on how much these past events might be playing into your present.

Early Influences and Family Dynamics

Our family environment and peer relationships will influence how we experience the world. This can have both positive and negative implications for our self-esteem. As we saw in the story about my client Martin, many of our narratives come from our interactions with our parents or caregivers when we were children. In Martin's case, while his parents never explicitly told him he wasn't good enough, his perception of the favoritism they showed toward his brother started to impact how Martin viewed himself. And so his narrative became one of not being good enough.

How key figures interacted with us as children matters and, over the years, we've become increasingly aware of the impact our attitudes toward children can have on their developing brains and personalities. Research has shown the importance of touch and nurture in fostering healthy brain development in babies.[7] It highlights that people in neglectful environments can experience developmental delays and changes in how their brain develops. So, it's unsurprising that our self-esteem also inevitably forms in our formative years. As a psychotherapist, I observe that most of my clients, at some point in their therapy journey, talk about aspects of their childhood and

---

7   Gerhardt, S. (2024), *Why Love Matters: How Affection Shapes a Baby's Brain*. London: Routledge.

revisit the painful and happy memories that still have an influence on them in the present.

Social and Cultural Factors

We know that influences on our self-esteem can come from social and cultural factors too. People from lower socioeconomic backgrounds generally experience lower self-esteem, because socioeconomic factors affect a person's ability to take part in health activities, invest in housing, and manage stress effectively, for example. Those who live in deprived communities are exposed to the challenges of deprivation, which means they're more likely to adopt a scarcity mindset. A scarcity mindset means that when we view the world through a lens of lack, we perceive other people's successes as a threat to our own potential – this is an outlook based on the premise of there not being enough to go around for all.

The people you spend most of your time with can also influence your self-esteem. Similarly, when we're surrounded by poverty daily, we'll likely have lower aspirations and feel we can't achieve financial affluence. Huge stigma can also be attached to certain geographical areas. For example, I grew up in Radford, Nottingham. This area is renowned for high crime rates, poverty, and disadvantage. However, what many people miss can be the hidden gems of these communities. In my work, I've seen how communities can be labelled disadvantaged but burst with unseen strengths. A strong sense of community and bonding is one of the positive elements of living in such areas. That said, it's more likely that people living in these areas will suffer the negative consequences of stigma, poverty, and shame, consequently lowering their self-esteem.

At the opposite end of the spectrum, I've encountered clients from more affluent backgrounds. These clients share how their experiences with private education taught them confidence – they were taught how to act and appear confident in posture, talk, and assertiveness – and yet, despite being very good at displaying this to the world on the surface, deep down they don't feel confident at all. Their levels of self-esteem appear to be equally impacted by having to pretend to be this self-assured, confident person, masking their true emotions and not being able to fully express who they are.

Race and Identity

Through the centuries, we have witnessed generations experience negative stereotypes and racial inequalities. It becomes impossible for people who have internalized messages of incompetence and inadequacy in society to go unscathed on a psychological level. When the dominant culture mistreats minorities, those affected internalize and accept these messages. This process is known as 'internalized racism.' We know that negative beliefs about one's racial group can contribute to low self-esteem, impact a person's mental health, and lead to negative narratives. The internal conflict is exacerbated further when you don't fit neatly into any racial category.

As a mixed-race woman, my experience of being born to parents of Black Jamaican and white British descent can bring up conflicting emotions and a sense of not belonging anywhere, as I've mentioned. I know this isn't true logically and in moments of higher self-esteem, but, at times, when low self-esteem grips me, I can return very quickly to these negative automatic thoughts. Research has shown that ethnic minorities often idolize the dominant culture and see themselves as inferior.[8] Many of these internal battles will be at a subconscious level as much as at a conscious level.

---

8   Prochaska, J. O. and Norcross, J. C. (2007), *Systems of Psychotherapy: A Transtheoretical Analysis*. Oxford: Oxford University Press.

Comparison and Social Media

In this digital age, we're often tempted to measure ourselves and our lives against others; it seems almost unavoidable when access to other people's lives is at our fingertips daily on our phones. The natural urge we have as humans is to be curious and we can't resist a sneaky peek at our friends, families, or colleagues. We see the curated experiences portrayed and the presumably perfect lives of celebs and influencers on social media. It's no wonder this can take a toll on our mental health, when we feel like our own lives or we ourselves just don't measure up. This starts to play into the narratives we tell ourselves.

As a therapist, I witness the impact this can have on my clients and how comparison can really drag people down. It contributes to the narratives they tell themselves – such as not feeling good enough, feelings of failure or jealousy – and this can lead to a sense of inadequacy, low self-esteem, and even depression.

They say comparison is the thief of joy, and it's true. The more we measure ourselves against others, the more we:

- lose sight of our own accomplishments
- sabotage our self-worth
- overlook the positive aspects of our own lives

We also run the risk of pushing others away. If comparison leaves you feeling dissatisfied with your own life, it may unintentionally make your loved ones feel like they're not enough either.

This doesn't mean that you shouldn't have ambition or set yourself goals. But you mustn't feel pressurized to attain achievements based on other people's perceived achievements or on your own sense of inadequacy or expectation.

It's helpful to remember that we all have unique journeys, and the life others portray on social media isn't always an accurate or complete picture of their daily existence. The stories, reels, and highlights that are shared are often carefully selected and designed to entice us and showcase the most exciting and opulent parts of their lives and, in some cases, are entirely fabricated.

Today, social media has become universally accepted as a normal part of most people's lives, but you can't tell me that it's never influenced you. Come on, be honest. I think all of us, even the most confident and self-assured people, have been impacted at some point by social media and we must acknowledge how this can influence our self-esteem story.

Constant exposure to curated representations of others' lives can fuel feelings of inadequacy and negatively impact self-esteem. For years, I enjoyed social media. I was one of the first-generation Facebook users when the company grew exponentially in 2008. I shared snippets of my life. It felt fun, and I enjoyed looking at other people's lives. However, I've also been through periods when I was aware of how it was impacting my thoughts and mood. So, I decided that social media wasn't healthy for me and stopped looking at Facebook and posting on it altogether. This has changed in recent years. Now that I run my online businesses, I admit it's a fantastic tool, but it becomes more beneficial when used with intention and purpose.

I frequently hear from my clients that social media use negatively impacts their self-esteem. They're aware of the narratives they tell themselves in relation to social media – such as feeling their life falls short compared to their friends' or feeling unwanted when they see friends socializing and having fun without them. If they're starting to feel this impact, I encourage them to make healthier choices regarding their social media use. This can include simple measures including:

- turning off notifications
- limiting phone use time
- having a phone detox (essentially, leaving your phone alone for an hour or two – the longer the better!)

I'm sure you have heard of these solutions before, but have you consciously committed to trying them?

I urge you to take a conscious approach to using social media. Observe how you feel when you use it, so you can start to make the same kind of links that I and many of my clients have. Does using social media leave you with a good, positive mindset? Or does it leave you feeling self-conscious and unhappy – essentially crap about yourself? As your self-esteem grows, you may be more immune to the impacts. I'm now aware that when my self-esteem was lower in the past, my struggles with social media lay at the heart of it, for it had become impossible not to compare myself to others.

You have a choice: You can engage in social media, but you don't have to. Social media can be an amazing tool that connects us with many people and allows us to converse with individuals we might have never met otherwise, building communities that share like-minded interests. However, we must also realize its impact on us. Be aware of what messages you're feeding your subconscious mind when indulging in social media fixes.

Critical Life Events

Significant life events can also have a lasting impact on self-esteem and the narrative you tell yourself. A critical life event may include trauma, bullying, or rejection.

Many people are unaware of how their past traumas are affecting them. They may not make the connection between past events and their current emotional state. They're oblivious to the control these events have over them – the sadness, anger, fear, or frustration. They feel the emotion, but haven't made the links between the present and those past experiences that are still affecting them. My role as a therapist is to help unearth these hidden layers. Therapy is powerful because it helps clients understand more deeply the impact these events have on them. We can achieve better levels of awareness by participating in activities to guide a deeper understanding of the self, and giving ourselves time to be on our own to engage in some soul-searching to reflect and help ourselves to heal. This book is a great starting point, and the exercises in it will help you do this.

Natalie's Story

I frequently see clients who have endured a significant life event that has had a lasting impact on their self-esteem. Natalie, 39, came to therapy due to her depression and anxiety. This had been a familiar occurrence throughout her life. She had seasons of better mental health and periods of lower mood and depression. She had endured the painful experience of her mum dying when she was 15 years old. Soon after, her dad entered a new relationship. His new partner wasn't nurturing toward Natalie and this immensely impacted her self-worth and esteem. The trauma of experiencing such painful grief at a young age is enough to make anyone to retreat into their shell, along with leaving them with feelings of abandonment and the fear of losing a key attachment figure in their life.

Natalie married in her 20s and found a sense of identity as a wife and mother, but she stepped back and allowed her husband to grow in his career. As a result, she shrunk into the background of life, feeling low self-worth and unfulfilled. When we worked together, she was able to explore her narrative and make the connections that had led to her lack of self-esteem. After months of commitment to therapy and changing her life, her self-esteem blossomed. She began to study after years of being in the same job. She even pursued a new career change, started a new hobby, and felt happier in her marriage.

INNER CHILD WORK

As we've seen, it's common for our most painful early experiences to be carried with us into adulthood. Some of my clients feel emotionally stuck at the age when they experienced the trauma, which has played a huge part in them developing low self-esteem. To move forward, they need to process these experiences before they can progress and heal emotionally.

It can be helpful to think of your inner child as those parts of your subconscious mind that still hold the childhood experiences you encountered. This can include good and bad memories. Acknowledging this inner child is a helpful tool when thinking about your narrative and the experiences you've been through. Once you become attuned to your inner child being activated or triggered, you can learn to soothe this part of yourself.

The therapist and educator John Bradshaw and the late Louise Hay were both pioneers of inner child work. This approach helps us to understand that we first see the world through the eyes of a child and that our 'inner child' remains with us throughout our lives. It helps us to understand that if, as a child, we felt vulnerable, hurt, abandoned, shamed, or neglected, that child's pain, grief, and anger live on within us. There are ways in which you can help heal your inner child, such as with meditation techniques. This can help you work through the coping mechanisms you've developed so you can finally connect with your true, authentic self. The exercise on pages 48–49 will help you to reflect on how your past experiences have contributed to your present self-esteem narrative.

THE ORIGINS OF MY NARRATIVE

At around the age of 10, I started to endure bullying at school because of my weight. I recall feeling mortified when the school required us to step on the scales, as others could see how much we weighed. I felt so vulnerable when people started to call me heavy and fat. This was the seed that started to grow into me feeling inherently flawed, and that narrative continued into my late teens and early twenties.

This led to me entering unhealthy relationships, not honoring my body, and seeking external validation in the form of approval from the opposite sex as a teenager. Then the narrative became even more consolidated when I was cheated on in a relationship when I was still a teen. From then on – and for such a long time afterward – I told myself that I wasn't worthy of being in a happy, loving, and committed relationship. I felt that I wasn't good enough to be truly loved.

Another narrative I told myself was that I was a bad person. I held a lot of shame around my experiences of shoplifting as a teenager. I tried to turn my life around after the shoplifting incidents, getting a job in a clothing shop. However, only weeks into the job, a security guard who had caught me several months earlier recognized me. Although I had now reached a point where I knew I wanted to change my ways and had no more intentions to shoplift, the shop owners weren't prepared to continue my employment, so my job was terminated. I felt I had let my family down. I was overwhelmed by a deep sense of shame and was convinced that my siblings were better and more lovable than me. I felt like the odd one out; I was the bad one who did things wrong and would never succeed in life. I held this belief for many years.

The layers of inadequacy also stemmed from the fact that I hadn't been to university. I felt a deep sense of just not being good enough. I compared myself to others and often didn't feel like I fitted in anywhere. This was all compounded by my mixed heritage. Sometimes, I was able to view my mixed heritage as a positive in that maybe I have the best of both worlds, but, mostly, I felt conflicted that I'd never really fitted in the white side of my family or the Black side. This was further extended to my peer relationships and trying to find where I fitted in there, too. How I presented myself, what music and clothes I should wear, and essentially who I was were all things I was trying to understand. These internal conflicts caused me a lot of emotional pain and fed my self-loathing. They limited me in life, made me feel undeserving, and had a substantial negative impact on my well-being, self-esteem, and levels of happiness.

It can be difficult to overcome such deep-rooted beliefs, but it is possible. It takes time and, even now, there will be moments when those old narratives resurface for me. The difference now is that I'm armed with more knowledge and a genuine conviction that even if, at times, I still don't feel enough, I know deep down I am.

I'm sure many of you reading this will be able to resonate with some of my stories. Yours will be unique to you, but if you've ever experienced low self-esteem, you will be able to empathize. In this exercise, we'll look at the key moments when your narrative began.

Your Self-Esteem Narrative Timeline

I would like you to consider any key moments in your life when your personal narrative may have been impacted.

1. Make a timeline by drawing a line on a piece of paper. (I personally love to use the huge rolls that you can get from IKEA for this exercise.) Write your date of birth at one end and your current age at the other.

2. Now, bearing in mind the influences we've discussed, I would like you to take some time to reflect on significant events or periods – both positive and negative – where your perspective, beliefs, or life direction changed. Plot these events in chronological order on your timeline.

3. When you've finished, reflect on why these moments are significant and how they influenced your narrative:

   - What emotions do these moments bring up?

   - How did each point shape who you are now?

   - If a similar situation arose today, would you respond differently?

This exercise will help you to pinpoint significant events, choices, and influences that have contributed to your narrative.

Reflecting on significant events in our lives may bring up strong emotions. This is a little reminder that if you're struggling with memories or feel distressed by things that come up, always seek support from a qualified mental health professional.

....

HOW YOU MAINTAIN YOUR NARRATIVE

Negative core beliefs perpetuate your narrative. Core beliefs are the deep-rooted ideas we have about ourselves, others, and the world in which we live. They guide our thinking about everything else and drive the surface thoughts that we experience. Core beliefs determine how we perceive and interpret the world, and can be positive, negative, or neutral. For example, you may believe you're a good or bad person. Others may feel that they are unlovable or loved, stupid or clever. As you can see, people with differing core beliefs will experience their worlds very differently.

Core beliefs are often a result of the narrative we've come to believe about ourselves – they have their roots in the messages we learned from our childhood, peers, family members, teachers, the media, wider stigmas, prejudice, and societal conditioning. The core beliefs we live by can lead us to internalize negative messages. Based on our experiences and how we interpret them, we conclude that we're unlovable, stupid, or not good enough. We can hold these beliefs very strongly in both the conscious and unconscious, and we can carry them into adulthood in the way we analyze and respond to day-to-day events. They can show up as avoiding situations, staying in relationships we aren't happy in, or holding ourselves back from experiences due to fear of failure – those avoidance behaviors and coping strategies we looked at in the last step (*see pages 15–22*). Once again, past experiences can lead to the emotional distress that you experience in the present.

Our negative core beliefs often serve as the foundation for low self-esteem. As a result, we tend to remember only things that happen in our lives that are consistent with what we believe to be true. This process of attending to and interpreting things in a manner that is consistent (rather than inconsistent) with our beliefs is something all human beings do, not just those with problems of low self-esteem, but acknowledging it helps us to realize the issues that can arise when we interpret ourselves as not being worthy. We analyze our interactions in life with a critical eye, internalizing ourselves as the problem.

When I look back now, I realize I held the core belief in my early 20s that I wasn't good enough. I felt flawed. It felt as if something was wrong with me. In my job as a receptionist at a secondary school, I felt like I was at the bottom of the pile. I was one of the lowest paid, but the responsibility of working at the front desk was on me – being the one to complete the demands placed on me day after day after day. It chipped away at my self-esteem and exacerbated the core belief I'd clung to from past rejections: memories from childhood, experiences of bullying and cheating, and the present-day unhappiness I was dealing with.

My core belief was this: *I'm flawed, I'm not worthy, I'm unlovable, and I'm a failure.* These messages I told myself every day led to my feelings of depression. In fact, I hated myself. I didn't respect myself, which ultimately made me unable to face the world anymore. I was ill and I had to take some time off work. It was during this time that I started my therapy, which not only led to my own healing, but helped me find my true calling to become a therapist myself.

Core beliefs can be hard to shift, but it's important to understand that our beliefs are in our control. Regardless of our narrative, we can decide how we let our life experiences shape who we are or want to become. The key here is to realize that these negative core beliefs aren't facts. You may currently believe that you aren't good enough or a failure, but that doesn't mean it's a fact. The following exercise will help you to identify and rewrite past negative or limiting stories that may still influence your present mindset.

What Is the Narrative You Tell Yourself?

Reflecting on and understanding what stories from the past are still influencing you today is a crucial step toward understanding how you might be holding on to negative or limiting beliefs about yourself.

1. Firstly, choose an event from your timeline that had a lasting impact on you. This may be something you believe has shaped your self-perception or life choices. It might be a difficult memory, a failure, or a relationship issue – any event you feel has influenced the narrative you tell yourself. For example:

    I was bullied at school.

2. Now, write down a detailed account of the event. Explore how you felt:

    - What emotions did you experience?
    - What thoughts did you have?
    - How did you interpret what had happened to you at the time?

3. Identify what story you started telling yourself as a result of this event. For example:

    I felt upset that the bully took my dinner money. I felt scared and I felt unlikeable. I felt worthless and I felt sad. I started to tell myself that no one liked me and that I wasn't a person worth being around; I didn't feel I was good enough. I also felt weak and stupid.

4. When reflecting on the story you wrote down, identify the core belief it created. It may be a belief about yourself or how you view others or the world. For example:

    I'm not good enough; I can't trust anyone.

5. Write down how this narrative or belief has affected you in your life since the event. Consider its influence on your relationships, career, self-esteem, and decisions. How has this story held you back or caused you pain? For example:

    It's made me cautious about who I can trust and make friends with. It's affected my self-esteem; I don't feel good enough. It's caused me to feel negative about myself, which has led to me getting into unhealthy relationships and seeking validation from others.

6. Question the accuracy and fairness of the narrative you've been telling yourself. Ask yourself:

    - Was this belief based on facts or just a reaction to the situation?
    - Could there be alternative explanations for what happened?
    - How would a compassionate friend or outsider view this event?

7. Write down these reflections. For example:

The belief that I'm not good enough and can't make friends is a reaction to the situation rather than a fact. Maybe this person who bullied me was unhappy herself and took it out on me. Maybe she didn't have a loving and supportive family to instill the same values in her like I did, as I would never treat anyone the way she treated me. A friend would remind me of my worth and also help me to see the positive qualities I have and bring to the friendships I have.

8. Following these reflections, rewrite the story from a more balanced, compassionate, and empowering perspective. Focus on how you have grown from that experience, what you have learned, and whether you developed any strengths or positive qualities out of it. For example:

   Instead of 'I'm a failure,' the new narrative might be, 'I faced a difficult challenge and my past experiences were painful, but this experience has helped shape who I am. It's influenced my decision to support others who may have been through similar experiences. It's been empowering to know that my values differ from the person who bullied me and I'm proud of who I am. I'm a kind, caring, and sensitive person. I use the past to empower me to become the best version of myself. I create a life that makes me feel happy and content. I know that the past experiences were due to the bully's own struggles and not a reflection of who I am. I am whole, I am worthy, and I let go of the past and know that it doesn't have a hold on me anymore.'

What is your narrative, and how is this still playing out in your life today? This exercise can be incredibly healing and help you to start unravelling and changing your narrative. Some issues may be deeply ingrained stories and, while this book will help you start to process them, it's not a replacement for therapy. Always seek professional help from a qualified mental health professional if you're struggling to process events from the past or present.

....

In Step 3, we'll take this exercise further and discover how to change your mindset, but, for now, let's look at something else that can give us a deeper insight into our narrative: our attachment style.

UNDERSTANDING YOUR ATTACHMENT STYLE

An attachment style, in short, is how we relate to and form relationships with others. Learning about your attachment style can help you better understand how you connect to others and how they connect to you. It can help explain why you may feel certain emotions, good and bad, and enable you to feel more in control of them when they arise. Identifying your attachment style can also help you understand how this shapes the narratives you tell yourself.

Pioneers in the field of counseling and psychotherapy, John Bowlby and Mary Ainsworth both researched into and wrote extensively about attachment theory.[9] Ainsworth's Strange Situation Experiment study, published in 1978, concluded that there are four main attachment styles:

1. An **anxious style** may manifest itself in relationships as someone who needs close proximity a lot of the time. They may need to feel close and become anxious when not with their partner or when they feel their relationship is under threat. They may fear that their partner doesn't want to get as close to them

---

9   Ainsworth, M. D. S. and Bell, S. M. (1970), 'Attachment, Exploration, and Separation: Illustrated by the Behavior of One-year-olds in a Strange Situation,' *Child Development*, 41: 49–67.

as they do, and they can be hypersensitive to tuning in to what their partner's facial cues are.

2. An **avoidant style** shows up as someone feeling uncomfortable when they start to get close in relationships. They may avoid closeness and tend to be more closed to emotion. They may not find it easy to open up in relationships.

3. A **disorganized style** is a combination of the anxious and avoidant attachment styles. Here, a person can present as having both high anxiety and high avoidance in relationships.

4. A **secure style** means that warmth and loving come easily. People with a secure attachment style tend to feel secure in relationships and don't generally experience jealousy.

As human beings, we were born to form relationships with others. This keeps us safe from harm when we're babies. When we grow older, this need to belong and feel loved remains the same – it's innate. As humans, we seek contact in the form of our relationships and ultimately want to feel loved and wanted. We strongly desire to belong in the world and connect to one another. Recognizing your attachment style can help you understand your behavior in your relationships, and having this awareness can help you to reflect on and modify any behaviors that are problematic. For example, if you tend to feel jealous and insecure in a relationship, you may have an anxious attachment style and fear that your partner will leave you. Your narrative may be that no one can love you or that you can't trust anyone. With this awareness, you can do something about this to improve your experience of the relationship. This may be to open up about this with your partner and have a conversation with them to understand why you may have these feelings.

Or maybe you get scared of intimacy in a relationship, emotional or physical, and this may mean you have an avoidant attachment style. This could play into narratives of not wanting to get close to someone because you feel scared of commitment or being hurt in the relationship. It's easier to just avoid strong emotions and commitment. This can make you pull away from a relationship, as you feel overwhelmed. For many of my clients, having this new-found awareness can help them to modify their behavior and respond in different ways, which can enable them to build stronger relationships and work through some of barriers they once faced.

Having a secure attachment style usually means people feel secure in their relationships and, as a result, relationships can be easier for these people.

Whatever your attachment style, it doesn't mean one is right and another is wrong. It just helps us understand how we relate to one another. If you've noticed recurrent patterns in your relationships that have been challenging or caused you distress, you may want to examine your attachment style. This can provide insights into the reasons behind these patterns. Knowing this can help you change problematic behaviors and avoid making the same mistakes. Likewise, it may help you to understand other people's attachment styles and how these may have impacted your relationships with them.

So, if you've ever felt rejection from a parent, caregiver, or someone you were close to, remember this: It's not because there is something innately wrong with you. Try instead to adopt compassion toward yourself and the person in question, for they may have their own narrative that's impacting their ability to meet your needs. Let me make it clear here that I'm not condoning any behavior that has been abusive or neglectful. I'm only encouraging you to realize that this isn't because of your own level of worthiness. It's simply because humans are complex. We endure hardships and challenges that can impact our ability to form healthy behaviors within our relationships.

I remember some key moments in my life when I experienced rejection from a family member who, ordinarily, most people would have a close relationship with. I was only around eight years old at the time. I asked if I could have a sleepover at their house and they flat-out said, 'No!' This moment of rejection stayed with me for many years. I felt unloved. I didn't feel I was good enough. As an adult reflecting on my childhood, I now realize that the way love was expressed within my family, coupled with the experiences of being bullied by my peers, played a huge part in shaping my self-perception during those formative years. I don't want to stereotype any group, because humans seldom fit into one box, but it's been widely acknowledged that Black Jamaican men, especially from the older generations, don't typically exhibit displays of affection and find it difficult to express their love verbally to their children. Often, this comes more naturally at the infant stage, but it becomes less easy with children aged 10 and above. I understand the ancestral trauma in my Jamaican bloodline, and the impact other familiar experiences such as loss and bereavement can have on people. Luckily, I experienced closeness with my dad. He showed his love in the way he knew how. For him, these were acts of care like picking me up from nursery, taking me to the park, taking me on day trips, and teaching me how to swim. His work ethic and ability to provide for our family have always been a big part of his identity and how he shows love. As I write this book, he still works as a doorman at the age of 72 for his own security company. I admire how his barriers have come down over the years, and how he can show love and affection to his six grandchildren. He often verbalizes his love for them, which is beautiful to witness.

While these acts of love were present, I still craved something more, especially as I grew older and became more aware of how parents could display love toward their children. My mother was more physically affectionate, sharing cuddles at bedtime, and showing care when she engaged in activities with me. Our household seldom said 'I love you' out loud, but I felt loved in many ways.

As a therapist, I now understand how attachment styles impact our human journey. We're complex beings, and we know that our ancestral story lines affect the way we were parented and how our parents' parents parented them. This can comfort some clients, who may feel their relationship with their parents is not as they desired. It takes the spotlight away from the client, enabling them to understand that our family history influences our attachment styles. Understanding these complexities can help us recognize how the narratives may start building in our minds. For example, if someone experienced harsh or punitive parenting, they may have narratives of not feeling good enough. If they weren't shown affection or told they were loved, their narrative may be that they're unlovable. Part of my role as a therapist is helping my clients rewrite some of the old narratives they once told themselves. Looking more into attachment theory can sometimes bring up deeper issues and emotions. This is especially true for those who may have had difficult childhoods. If this is the case for you, seeking help in therapy can be one way to assist you in exploring your feelings about this.

YOU CHOOSE HOW YOU VIEW YOUR NARRATIVE

My aim in this step has been for you to build on the self-awareness you gained in the first step and understand how your history has shaped your present – how all the many experiences you've had until now have impacted how you feel about yourself. But there is one last lesson I want to leave with you right now and that's that *you* decide how you view your narrative.

Knowing you can view your narrative however you desire can be extremely empowering. You'll feel less worthy if you believe your story makes you less worthy. If you view your story as your strength, you will step into that strength. Of course, I know how deeply someone's narrative can hurt them, especially when it involves trauma, and, for many of my clients, this is often what brought them to therapy. But I also know that when my clients reframe how they view aspects of their narrative, they can see themselves in a different and more positive light. By focusing on how those experiences have shaped them into the unique person they are today, they can gain a new-found appreciation for their journey and a more optimistic outlook on their future.

You are not your story; that's simply a part of your unique journey to your higher self. When people allow their narrative to be the dictator of their outcomes in life, they live in a place of despair. They can't thrive or grow into their divine life purpose. Many clients enter therapy at a time when their lives have stagnated and they feel stuck, yet this is a choice they continue to make. My training in the field of social work has enabled me to have a deeper understanding of the huge injustices in the world: poverty, abuse, neglect, and generational trauma; they all play their part in making some people's life journey arduous. But I know from all the clients and wonderful people I've met in my work that each person has the same worth and potential, no matter their background, and they just need to allow themselves to tap into the pure potential that exists within us all.

For those who find this difficult to achieve, I've seen how it can play out in their lives, including examples of how somebody who decides to stay in an unhappy relationship chooses their story, while the person who decides to leave an unhealthy relationship has chosen their 'self.' The person who realizes that they're good enough to apply for another job, retrain for a different career, or take the leap to start their own business has similarly chosen to take control of their destiny. They're the decisive and bold individuals who are willing to take a leap and start a new course, leaving their job to recreate themselves. Whether it's a new hairstyle, reading a self-help book, learning a new skill, or buying a new outfit, they're willing to make the choice that's necessary for them. They're willing to stop putting themselves last and ditch the old narrative that told them they're not worthy, not good enough, or that they don't deserve to be happy. Are you willing to make that choice for yourself and put yourself first, too?

••••

We all have the power to transform our low self-esteem and step into our higher self. Throughout this book, we'll delve deeper into understanding how we can rewrite our narrative using the theories I've introduced in this step. This will enable you to have the tools to understand how your narrative impacts your self-esteem, so that you can view yourself in a much more positive light. The following therapeutic exercises will further help you to unravel your narrative and heal from painful childhood memories.

As a therapist, I need to say that negative self-perception is a common experience shared by many, so don't feel alone. As humans, we can reflect on our emotions and feelings, but when we have the core belief that we aren't good enough, this can significantly impact the quality of our lives. To get to a place where we can stop operating from the limited version of ourselves and step into our higher power, we must reject the old stories and become attuned to the inner chatter that keeps us in a self-perpetuating cycle of emotional self-abuse – and we'll be exploring this in the next step.

THERAPEUTIC EXERCISES

Self-Reflection and Journaling

Self-reflection is so important for strengthening our relationship with ourselves and understanding how our narrative impacts us. It can give us more clarity and understanding and help us transform our self-esteem story. Here are some journal prompts to help guide you in exploring and challenging your narrative:

- What is a negative story you tell yourself frequently? Where did this come from and is it based on facts or assumptions?

- How does this negative story you tell yourself benefit other people? Who would it benefit if you replaced it with a positive narrative instead?

- Write about a challenging experience from your past that significantly impacted your self-esteem. How has this experience shaped your self-perception and beliefs about yourself?

- Reflect on a recent situation where you felt proud of yourself. What strengths or qualities did you exhibit in that moment, and how did it affect your self-esteem?

Letter to Your Inner Child

1. Write a heartfelt letter to your younger self (your inner child), offering words of encouragement, support, and wisdom.

2. Remember, your inner child is still a part of you. Reflect on how your past experiences have contributed to your present self-esteem narrative.

3. Acknowledge and validate their experiences and emotions. Imagine you're writing to a child you deeply care for with empathy, understanding, and compassion. You can also let your inner child 'respond' with a letter back to you if you want to.

It can be helpful to write letters to your younger self at different ages and at specific periods of your life when things were particularly challenging or had a big impact on you.

Understanding Your Narrative Guided Meditation

1. Make yourself comfortable. Close your eyes if this feels comfortable for you and focus on your breath. As you focus on your breath, breathe deeply and slowly. Stay like this for a few moments until you enter a deep state of relaxation.

2. I want you to bring to your attention an old narrative you've been clinging to. This may be a negative belief you've held about yourself for a long time, such as unworthiness, shame, guilt, or fear.

3. Create this vision of the old narrative in your mind. How does it make you feel? Notice what emotions arise and how this feels within your body.

4. Now, place this old narrative in front of you: You may visualize the words or images as if they were in front of you or on paper. See these words or pictures representing this old narrative you've been clinging to. Please take a moment to acknowledge this old story and then visualize yourself

walking away from it, knowing that this narrative no longer defines you; you're more than this old story.

5. Visualize the piece of paper with the old narrative on it. See the words and images on the paper start to fade away. This fading represents your power to release the old stories you used to tell yourself. Let go of all the negative beliefs that were tied to this old narrative and know that you are more than this.

6. As the old narrative fades, the paper allows for new stories to be written. A blank canvas is created and you have the power to write a new narrative for yourself. A story full of abundance, potential, compassion, strength, and infinite possibilities. What does this narrative look like? What feelings and emotions arise with the new narrative? What words and affirmations resonate with the person you're becoming? With each step you take, you walk closer to the new story you're creating. Let these new stories and positive affirmations start to sink into every cell of your being.

7. With your new story written, I want you to visualize it becoming a part of you. How does your body respond to this new story of abundance, potential, and compassion? Notice any changes in your breathing, posture, and energy. Allow yourself to fully embody this new story, letting it shape every action and interaction with others.

8. Repeat to yourself silently or out loud, 'I am the author of my own story. I choose to write a narrative of self-love, strength, and abundance. I release the old and embrace the new narrative I create each day.'

9. Take a few more deep breaths, embedding this affirmation into your heart. When you feel ready, slowly bring your awareness back to the present moment. Open your eyes if they were closed, stretch if you want to, and then go on with your day.

10. Carry this sense of rebirth and empowerment with you. Remember that you have the power within to rewrite your story and believe in your potential.

....

Affirm:

I can rewrite my narrative and cultivate a positive self-esteem story.

REJECT OLD STORIES

Step 3

The third step involves rejecting the old stories from the past and creating new, more balanced ways of seeing the world.

In the last step, we started to unravel your narrative. Now, it's time to reject those old stories you've been telling yourself and reframe your mindset so you can step into a more balanced way of viewing yourself and the world.

UNDERSTANDING NEGATIVE THINKING PATTERNS

In therapy, one recurring theme I see with my clients is negative thinking patterns, which happen when we make incorrect assumptions, engage in self-criticism, and deny the reality of situations. Negative thinking patterns stem from the underlying negative core beliefs we explored in the previous step (*see pages 49–51*). They can dictate the way we feel toward ourselves and determine the decisions and actions we take in life.

Negative thinking patterns are automatic and self-critical beliefs and assumptions, and it's these thoughts that keep us from being able to build healthy perceptions of ourselves. They're normally distorted views that don't reflect reality and impair our emotional well-being, because the thoughts lead to feelings of inadequacy, anxiety, depression, and a ubiquitous sense of dissatisfaction with our lives. It's not uncommon for people to experience these thoughts, and they're at the heart of many of the issues that I help people with in therapy. These thoughts can subtly interfere with our daily lives and affect our decisions, actions, and self-esteem.

I see people operating as a limited version of themselves all the time. I witness clients who predict the future, ruminate about issues that never come to fruition, and think negative things about themselves that are *not true,* causing them deep feelings of unhappiness. At their most destructive, these thoughts can lead to self-harm and suicidal ideas. We can't underestimate the toxicity of these negative thoughts and ruminations, which can harm our emotional health and limit our capacity to reach our full potential and live the lives we truly desire. On that note, I urge any of you experiencing suicidal thoughts to get help by visiting your healthcare provider or a mental health professional. People experience suicidal thoughts more commonly than you're probably aware of, and it's key to seek support.

People with low self-esteem are stuck in patterns of negative thinking, which simply maintain their narrative – it's often a case of them proving themselves right about the negative perceptions they have about themselves, because they're stuck and don't know how to get out of the loop. When we experience negative thinking patterns, we can constantly doubt our abilities or worth, leading to destructive internal dialogue. The inner voice that tells you that you aren't good enough or worthy enough can be an emotional drain.

Most of us experience negative thinking patterns now and again. This is normal and part of being human. However, it becomes more problematic when these negative thinking patterns become so ingrained within our psyche that they interfere with our relationships, daily activities, and well-being. I often see clients who don't realize how much these negative thinking patterns affect their lives, so let's now look at how you can identify them in your own life.

IDENTIFYING CLOUDY THOUGHTS

One of the most helpful tools we can arm ourselves with is identifying our negative thinking patterns, also known as cognitive distortions. This often catalyzes the positive changes I witness in my clients' lives. When they become more aware of their negative thinking patterns and how those thoughts impact their daily lives, they can take control of them, and challenge their limited perceptions of how they view the world.

I've listed some of the most common negative thinking patterns here. As you read through them, I urge you to reflect on whether any particular one of these resonates more with you than others. It can be helpful to name these thoughts as 'cloudy' and 'clear.' Cloudy thoughts are the thoughts that are often distorted and make us feel negative. Clear thoughts are the more balanced ways of seeing the world. Put a tick against any cloudy thoughts that you regularly experience.

Mental Filter

This is when we only notice the bad things and filter out the positives of a situation, seeing things from a negative perspective.

Cloudy thought: I'm not as successful as my friends are.

Clear thought: Can I look at some of the positives instead?

Mind-Reading

This is when we guess what others are thinking.

Cloudy thought: No one likes me.

Clear thought: Is there another way of looking at the situation?

Prediction

This is when we think we can predict the future.

Cloudy thought: I'm never going to achieve my goals.

Clear thought: How likely is it that this might really happen?

Compare and Despair

This is when we compare ourselves to others, have feelings of hopelessness, or are in a state of despair.

Cloudy thought: They're so pretty, and I'm so ugly and unattractive! I will never be in a relationship.

Clear thought: Could there be a more balanced/helpful way of looking at this situation?

Critical Self

This is when we're self-critical.

Cloudy thought: I can't do anything right!

Clear thought: What would people I know and respect say to me?

Should and Musts

This is when we put more pressure on ourselves than needed.

Cloudy thought: This must be perfect! I should have all of the rooms in the house tidy before my guests come round. I should be better than this!

Clear thought: What would be more realistic?

Judgments

This is when we make a judgment about an event or a person.

Cloudy thought: Everyone in the room will think I'm stupid.

Clear thought: Is there another perspective?

Emotional Reasoning

This is when we use our emotions (how we feel) to make a decision about something.

Cloudy thought: I feel bad, so it must be bad.

Clear thought: My feelings are just an automatic reaction, but I don't have to keep looking at it this way.

Mountains and Molehills

This is when we exaggerate and make mountains out of molehills.

Cloudy thought: Everyone hates me! I'm useless and stupid and no one will talk to me because I'm such a failure.

Clear thought: How would someone else see it? What's the bigger picture?

Catastrophizing

This is when we think about the worst thing that could happen and assume it will.

Cloudy thought: I'll never find a job – no one will ever employ me!

Clear thought: Are there other outcomes that could happen here?

Black-and-White Thinking

This is when we tend to think in extreme ways – extremely negative or extremely positive!

Cloudy thought: I'm going to fail miserably at my driving test!

Clear thought: There are shades of grey, too. What else could be at play in a situation?

Memories

This is when we base our thoughts on past events.

Cloudy thought: I always fail at everything. I wasn't clever at school; I'll never be good at anything because of this.

Clear thought: Even though I feel triggered, it doesn't mean that this is the same as what happened in the past. This is now, not then.

••••

I encourage you to become more aware of these negative thinking patterns and how they manifest in your life. Over the next week, observe the cloudy thoughts that pop into your head. These are often automatic negative ways of thinking, and they can be so automatic that we can accept these thoughts without challenge – but now you're raising your awareness even further. I encourage you to write down every cloudy thought, no matter how small. It's essential to keep track. The key here is to be aware of how often you have them. After a week of reviewing your thoughts, are there any recurring themes and patterns in your self-criticism? Let's dive a bit deeper now with an exercise.

Reflect – Identify – Challenge

Challenging your cloudy thoughts can have a significant impact on your self-esteem and self-image, and help you to recognize how self-critical thoughts lead to the narrative you tell yourself, reinforcing behaviors and outcomes. Here's how:

1. **Reflect:** At the end of each day, jot down a situation where you felt 'not good enough' or disappointed in yourself.

2. **Identify:** For each situation, write down three things:
   - Thought: What did I think about myself?
   - Behavior: How did I act because of this?
   - Outcome: What happened?

3. **Challenge:** After a few entries, look back and ask yourself, 'How would things have gone differently if I'd responded differently?' This can help you to learn new, more positive ways of viewing situations.

One of my favorite quotes by the esteemed Louise Hay is: 'Every thought we think is creating our future.'[10] This is one of the simplest but most potent pieces of information I can arm you with. This is because when we consciously become aware of how frequently our negative thoughts impact our lives, we can do something about it and start to reframe how we view situations, reject the old stories, and improve our outlook on ourselves and life in general. This can help us make better decisions from a place of assurance and feel confident in our abilities.

---

10 Hay, L. (1994), *You Can Heal Your Life*. London: Hay House, p.7.

When you live from your limited self, you're governed by the negative narrative you have been telling yourself – the narrative that stops you from reaching your full potential, keeps you accepting less than you are worth, and leaves you stuck in situations you aren't happy with. When you learn to live from your higher self, you can do things differently. You will feel more fulfilled and content, knowing that you're acting from the part of you that isn't governed by ego but led by your spirit or soul. When you learn to tap into this part of you, you can overcome the ego's advances that stop you from doing what you truly desire. The higher self disregards previous narratives and considers the past essential for development.

Your Limited Versus Your Higher Self

Use these journal prompts to identify when you are listening to your limited self, versus your higher self:

- How often do you listen to your limited self? How does this impact your quality of life?

- How frequently do you listen to your higher self? How would it impact your life if you listened to this part of you more often?

Mohammed's Story

Mohammed, a 42-year-old business analyst, had struggled with depression and anxiety for several years. We discovered in therapy that his depression stemmed from the negative, self-limiting thoughts he experienced. These thoughts had a significant impact on his personal and professional life. As a result, this further exacerbated his feelings of inadequacy and anxiety.

Mohammed often doubted his abilities, making him anxious about taking on new challenges at work. This led to him turning down opportunities to advance his career, including two promotions his manager thought he would be a good fit for. His fear of stepping into a new role that felt out of his comfort zone was due to the extra responsibilities it would entail, which would mean having to manage staff and demonstrate leadership and the assertiveness to make independent decisions. The unknowns of this new role and the fear of failure kept him stuck in the same job for 10 years. This would be fine if he was happy, but he wasn't. Deep down, he longed to make a more significant impact, but his current job limited his ability to do so.

His limited self would tell him that he was incapable of leading a team, wouldn't excel at leading team meetings, and was rubbish at public speaking. His limited self also told him he didn't deserve the promotion anyway, because he still wasn't performing as well as he would like in some areas of his current role.

We started using cognitive behavioral techniques to help Mohammed better understand the frequency of his negative thoughts and how much they impacted his day-to-day life. Over several months, he became more positive in his outlook on life. He started to take on new challenges at work, improve his social skills, and prioritize his self-care.

With ongoing support and dedication to change, Mohammed started to live from his higher self more often than he did from his limited self, and subsequently lead a more fulfilling life.

While working with clients like Mohammed, I've seen how when they regularly listen to the negative dialogue that tells them they aren't good enough, not worthy, and flawed, these negative thinking patterns continue to embed feelings of low self-worth. The perpetuating cycle continues, and they feel more and more negatively toward themselves. But it *is* possible to break this cycle!

COGNITIVE RESTRUCTURING

Cognitive behavioral therapy (CBT) helps us understand more about how our thoughts impact our thinking patterns, and how we feel and behave as a result. CBT can help us understand our self-perception and the connection between our thoughts, feelings, and actions, and it can be a powerful tool to help us reject the old stories we tell ourselves.

I like to use a little analogy with my clients when introducing them to CBT approaches. I liken it to our brains being like our email inboxes. We receive hundreds of emails daily, but most are junk mail. To know which ones are worth keeping and which we need to discard, we must look at them. Similarly, CBT involves deciphering negative thoughts from healthy ones and reframing your thinking (the cognitive). This can help you respond differently, thereby modifying your behaviors. This can often lead to a profound shift in your well-being, offering a hopeful path toward a healthier mental state.

While acknowledging the impact of our past experiences on our present, CBT predominantly concentrates on enhancing our mental health in the present. The core message of CBT is that our emotions aren't shaped by the event itself, but by how we interpret it, the thoughts we entertain, and the meaning we give to situations. For example, in the case of low self-esteem, a person may have the thought 'If I get on this bus, everyone is going to think I'm stupid and ugly.' These thoughts make the person feel anxious and sad, and they may decide to avoid getting on the bus. This can perpetuate a harmful cycle of negativity and inactivity.

CBT empowers you with the tools to let go of old stories and break away from this negative thinking pattern. It enables you to challenge negative thoughts and instead adopt a healthier, more balanced way of seeing the world. You learn to question the voice telling you not to get on the bus. Instead of automatically accepting that everyone will judge you, CBT helps you pause, examine that thought and ask, 'Is this really true?' Over time, it enables you to board the bus – not because you're suddenly fearless, but because you've developed the ability to see your thoughts more clearly and respond to them more wisely. You learn that the bus isn't as threatening as it seemed, and that you don't have to let those old fears dictate your destination. This sense of empowerment can be a significant boost to your mental well-being.

I love teaching my clients CBT, because it's such a simple but effective tool that they can learn to use independently after our therapy sessions have concluded. And I want to arm you with the same knowledge so that you can use it, too.

Reframing Your Recurring Negative Thoughts

Here is a simple reframing exercise you can do when you're spiraling. Spiraling is when we overthink a situation and start to feel overwhelmed, or when we ruminate about the issue at hand over and over again.

So often, our automatic thoughts are negative and totally unfounded. The negative thinking patterns we experience help maintain low self-esteem. To break free from this cycle, we can follow a process to help us reframe the negative thoughts so we develop a more balanced way of seeing a situation.

Here are some examples of negative thoughts and then a more balanced/positive thought beside it.

Negative Thought	Balanced/Positive Thought
I can't do anything right.	Sometimes, I get things wrong, but that's OK; we all do.
I am going to be fired.	I am finding my job challenging, but I am doing my best.
I have no money.	I would like to have more money, but I'm grateful to have some.

Now, I would like you to create your own table, listing some of your most common negative thinking patterns in the first column and then reframing them into balanced/positive thoughts in the second column.

For many clients, reframing thoughts can feel like hard work at first. However, with practice and persistence, staying committed to the process, it'll become more automatic. This, in turn, will help increase your sense of well-being and improve how you view yourself.

....

Rejecting old stories means that you have to start seeing yourself through a different lens than you've ever done before. It is an ongoing process that, in my own experience, requires you to work on it daily. It can be so easy for us to keep that negative dialogue going in our minds – the one that when we look in the mirror tells us that we aren't attractive or that we're stupid or not worthy. Sometimes, these thoughts are so ingrained in us that we aren't fully aware of how often they happen. But the more we start to notice these thoughts, the more we can control them and change how we view ourselves.

Cognitive restructuring can help you become more aware of the negative thinking patterns you experience and, in turn, rethink how you view yourself. For example, one my clients kept having persistent **thoughts** of 'I'm not good enough.' This created **feelings** of low mood and anxiety, which then led to their **behavior** of withdrawing from social situations. The cycle of thoughts into feelings into behavior can turn into a vicious circle of negativity, as described by Dr. Aaron T. Beck and shown in this diagram.[11]

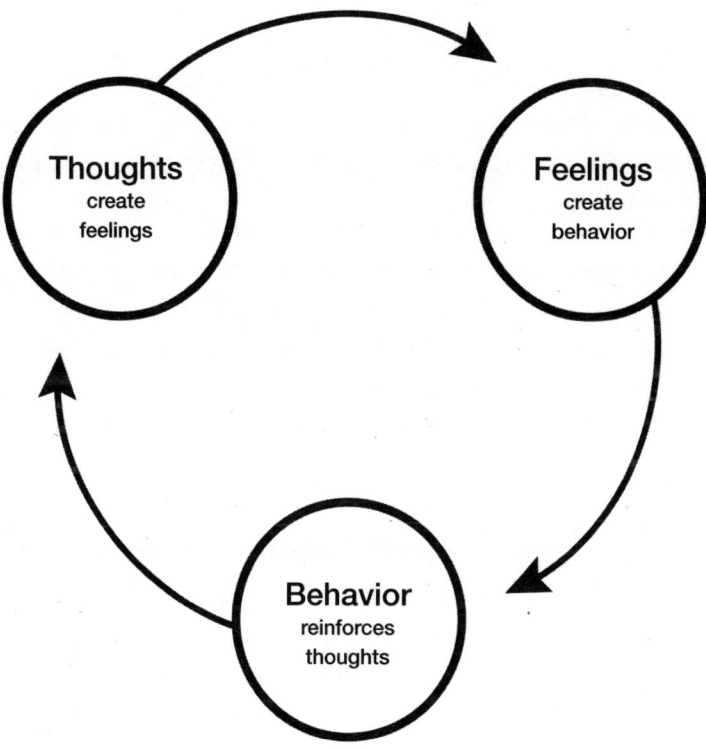

The Cycle of Negative Thinking Patterns

---

11   Beck, A.T. (1967), *Depression: Causes and Treatment*. Philadelphia: University of Pennsylvania Press.

1. **Thoughts:** Examining our thoughts like a detective can help us become more aware of how distorted some of our thinking can be. Being mindful of the thoughts that have entered your mind, what is making you feel uncomfortable, and what it means to you is crucial to understanding how you're interpreting situations. It's also helpful to remember that sometimes our thoughts may take the form of questions; for example, 'Do they think I'm stupid?' or 'Am I good enough?'

2. **Feelings:** CBT helps us understand that the emotions we feel are a direct consequence of our thoughts. When we experience negative thoughts, we encounter tricky emotions such as anxiety, anger, or low mood, for example. Being aware of our feelings can help us make connections between the thoughts fueling these emotions.

3. **Behavior:** Our behavior is then determined by the thoughts and feelings we have. This may significantly shape our actions and influence what we do in any given situation. For example, if you're feeling anxious, low, or angry, you will respond to the situation accordingly.

Reframing Specific Negative Thoughts

I would like you to reflect on a recent situation that made you angry, anxious, or in a low mood. Now, identify your thoughts about the situation and how this impacted your feelings and then your behavior.

Example of negative thought: *I'm useless.*

Example of feelings connected to the thought: anxiety and self-doubt

> **Example of behavior because of the thought:** avoiding trying new things for fear of failure

Now, try reframing negative thoughts with a more balanced/positive outlook. Is there a different way you could choose to view this thought?

> **Example of balanced/positive thought:** *I get some things wrong, but everyone does.*
>
> **Example of feeling now connected to this more balanced thought:** optimism
>
> **Example of behavior because of new thought:** willing to try new things and feeling OK when things go wrong

·················

Mindfulness and awareness techniques can play a useful role in cognitive restructuring. You may already be aware of mindfulness, which includes meditation, breathing, and yoga to help manage our thoughts, feelings, and bodily sensations. These exercises can help you to become more aware of your thoughts and be more present in the moment, which is incredibly helpful for rejecting intrusive or automatic negative thoughts. Mindfulness can also reduce the likelihood of relapsing into depression and anxiety, so it's a useful tool to incorporate into your daily life. To try it for yourself, I encourage you to do the Rejecting Old Stories Guided Meditation at the end of this chapter (*see pages 90–91*).

BUILDING POSITIVE SELF-TALK

One of my biggest drivers in life is to help other people step into their higher power and live the life they truly deserve (don't worry – all the steps in this book are leading up to that!). A potent tool you can use and have access to whenever you desire is positive self-talk. It's such a simple concept, but a powerful way to transform how you speak to yourself. It involves consciously connecting with the internal dialogue always playing in your mind. It can disrupt any of our negative thoughts that are on autoplay and change how we view ourselves, improving our self-esteem and general well-being.

There are many benefits of positive self-talk:

- It promotes self-confidence. Acknowledging our achievements helps us build the foundation for really believing in ourselves. We can rise to challenges and adopt a more resilient mindset, knowing we can succeed.

- It helps to activate our soothing system and encourages us to focus on more constructive thoughts, allowing us to manage stress more effectively. Positive self-talk can have a significant impact on reducing anxiety, too.

- It makes us more motivated and productive, because it's like having an inner cheerleader who encourages us to overcome life's hurdles and reach our goals and desires. With this positive chatter in our head, we're more likely to strive toward our goals and live a more fulfilled life.

- It improves our relationships. How we speak to ourselves impacts how we speak to those around us. When we talk positively to ourselves, we adopt a healthier self-image and feel good about ourselves, so we have more confidence. When we feel good about ourselves, a natural side effect is that we approach relationships with confidence, are more open, and can display compassion more easily toward others. This helps foster stronger relationships and connections.

- It improves our mind and body! Positive self-talk can improve the way we view life and how we approach it. When we use positive self-talk, we become more optimistic and realistic, which, in turn, improves our overall health and vitality.

What's not to love about positive self-talk?

So far, we've explored the destructive nature of negative self-talk. On the contrary, positive self-talk can have an amazing impact on rebuilding our relationship with ourselves. One way I've built a better relationship with myself is to honor my time, ensuring I have the opportunity each week to be alone, doing the things I enjoy. Positive self-talk has helped me change thoughts such as 'I should spend time with my family' to 'If I exercise for an hour at the gym, I'll have more energy and enjoyment when spending time with my family.' Positive self-talk is a kinder, more accepting way of talking to ourselves.

From my own battle with negative self-talk, I know that one of the times I experience relapse and return to my old ways of behaving is in situations when I get something wrong or have a disagreement with my husband. It can also occur when I feel like I've let down my children or haven't achieved something I wanted to achieve. That inner dialogue can quickly bring me back to berating myself and reflecting on the old narrative I used to believe. So, a word of reassurance for you on your journey: relapses and triggers are part of it. You should expect this to happen, but the further you get into your journey toward living from your higher self, the quicker you'll be able to bounce back and build resilience. Things simply won't affect you as much as they used to. You can recover quicker and have the tools to help yourself.

Now, let's dive into some top tips for improving your own self-talk.

Track Your Progress and Celebrate Successes

Journaling can be a powerful tool for tracking relapses and progress in negative self-talk. This can help you build awareness of any changes related to your low self-esteem. As with my clients, I encourage you to write down your thoughts and feelings regularly. This is particularly important when you're feeling down or tapping into negative self-talk. It can help you identify patterns, like recurring triggers or negative beliefs.

It's important to acknowledge your progress and celebrate your success. My clients have shared how beneficial it can be to start with small goals and build to bigger ones. For example, in the case of negative self-talk, you might set a small goal to start with, replacing one negative thought per day with a higher-self thought. When you meet a goal, celebrate it. It may be with a small treat or by sharing your success with someone in your support network (*see pages 86–87 for more about this*).

Practice Gratitude

One quality I have seen that helps clients in their quest for recovery is gratitude, when they start to track and become aware of what they appreciate in their lives. When low mood, depression, or anxiety take grip, it can be too easy to enter a rabbit hole of negative thinking, and this can distort our view of the world. I'm sure you may be familiar with gratitude, which involves regularly acknowledging and appreciating the good things in your life. When we do this, it naturally takes the focus away from the old stories we have been fixated on.

At times, I've felt guilty for becoming so obsessed with the things I want to attract into my life that I've overlooked the abundance I already have. This can be a slippery slope when we get into the mode of striving for more. Over the past few years, I've learned to remain focused on all I have in life, because I know that the younger version of myself would have been amazed at what I've accomplished. So, even if you aren't living the dream life you want to just yet, please take a moment to reflect on the positives you do have. There will be some, even if it doesn't seem like much. It may be more than others have at the moment and, for that, we can be grateful. It may be things such as your health, your family, your job, your warm bed, or a cooked meal. It may be the simplest of things we often take for granted. As I write this book, there are atrocities of war going on across the world. Take a moment to realize how much you have. It may be as simple as acknowledging the safety, food, and water – our most basic needs – that some people worldwide currently don't have.

Writing Positive Affirmations

For this exercise, I want you to create personalized affirmations reflecting positive beliefs about yourself and your abilities. I know this may feel strange if you're not used to praising yourself, but this is an important stepping stone toward a more positive mindset, helping you to reject the old stories you've told yourself for too long. So, even if you don't believe this just yet, take some time to write down what you would like to believe about yourself.

When choosing affirmations, I encourage you to use the words 'I am' at the start and repeat the affirmations daily to reinforce positive self-talk and boost your self-esteem. You may even want to write them down on sticky notes and put them on your bathroom or bedroom mirror; personally, I love to write affirmations down in my phone reminders so that they pop up at various parts of the day.

Some examples of positive affirmations include:

- I am capable.
- I am loved.
- I am strong.
- I am confident.
- I am deserving.
- I am ready to learn.
- I am ready to grow.

Now, practice writing some of your own affirmations.

·····················

Create a Support System

It can be really helpful to get people you love and trust on board to help you change and shift your negative thinking patterns. Loved ones often witness the negative things we say about ourselves and know us more intimately than most and see us when we're in our lowest moments. They hear us when we speak unkindly to ourselves and see the unhappiness we experience as a result. So, one thing that can be helpful is to share with those who you love and trust that you're committing to reduce the negative self-talk you use toward yourself. You may ask them to support you by flagging this when they hear you do it.

On the flip side of this, I also encourage my clients to build awareness of who makes them feel good and who makes them feel negative. Do you have people who tend to drain your energy or make you feel bad? When rejecting old stories, it's important to note how others influence your feelings. Reading through this book involves a lot of inner work, and you'll make significant shifts from the work you're putting in. It's essential to take steps to shield yourself from individuals who frequently make disparaging remarks, criticize you, or exhibit a negative outlook. However, it's also important to note that this doesn't mean that you should expect everyone to be constantly cheerful and carefree.

Kavita's Story

Kavita, 26 and a mother of two girls, sought therapy for ongoing feelings of low mood and anxiety. She described how she was unhappy with her appearance, felt she wasn't very clever, and didn't do well in school or college. She left college early and got a low-paid job that covered the bills but didn't inspire her. She felt she wasn't going anywhere in life, which profoundly impacted her overall well-being.

Her negative thinking patterns had become ingrained over the years, leading to a cycle of self-doubt, anxiety, and depression. She often compared herself to others, focusing on her perceived flaws and shortcomings. This negative self-talk affected her relationships, work performance, and parenting.

In one of her therapy sessions, Kavita shared an incident that sparked a significant realization. Her eldest daughter repeated a self-critical statement that Kavita frequently made about her own appearance. Hearing her words mirrored back by her child was a wake-up call for her. She realized that her negative self-talk wasn't only harming herself, but influencing her daughters' self-perception.

We worked on her negative thinking patterns and identified how her narrative impacted her feelings toward herself. The safe space that therapy provided for her helped her focus on fostering a positive environment for her daughters, promoting self-esteem and modeling healthy self-talk. She encouraged open communication and taught her children the importance of self-acceptance. Kavita's story is an inspiration to all of us who are struggling with similar challenges, emphasizing the importance of self-awareness, self-care, and resilience in overcoming negative thinking patterns. I hope this book will similarly serve as a safe space in which to identify the limitations you've been placing on yourself and to break free from them, thus allowing you to tap into your innate potential.

Practicing positive self-talk takes a concerted effort at first – we often have to unravel years of negative automatic thinking patterns. Be patient and compassionate toward yourself as you learn these new skills. Often, the small and consistent efforts we make can lead to significant improvements in our self-esteem and overall mindset.

••••

Remember, progress over perfection is key. I often remind my clients that they've clung to these negative self-perceptions for a long time, so we can't expect them to disappear overnight. It really is an ongoing process. The key is your commitment to rejecting old stories, as it's a lifelong journey. Keep moving forward and practicing the things you're learning in each step. By staying committed to the journey, you're building healthier self-esteem and fostering a deeper love for yourself than you've ever had before.

This leads us nicely to another important element of rejecting old stories: becoming your authentic self. In the next step, we're going to shift our focus onto more positive aspects of ourselves and being grateful for the skills, abilities, and unique qualities we possess.

THERAPEUTIC EXERCISES

Gratitude Journaling

For one week, I would like you to keep a gratitude journal.

A gratitude journal is where you write down all of the things that you appreciate. This is about focusing on the positive aspects of yourself and your life, which can help shift your mindset toward a more optimistic and appreciative outlook. That doesn't mean that everything is perfect, but it does mean that you're consciously giving yourself the time to focus on the personal qualities and things you have in your life that you feel grateful for.

Dealing with Failure and Mistakes

One aspect people with low self-esteem find difficult is when they make mistakes or fail at something. Of course, every human makes mistakes; none of us are perfect. However, low self-esteem can make us feel more intense emotions around failure. Negative thoughts are often activated, and a negative thinking loop begins. We'll all continue to make mistakes in our lives, and this has nothing to do with our worth; it's simply part of being human.

In the exercise on pages 80–81, you practiced reframing your thoughts. This exercise will build upon that, but you will specifically focus on when you make a mistake.

1. Make a list of all of the negative thoughts you experience when you make a mistake. For example:

    I'm stupid! or *I always get things wrong!*

2. Now, I want you to reframe how you see this mistake into a more balanced, compassionate way of viewing the situation. For example:

    I'm human and we all make mistakes sometimes!

We'll look in more detail at seeing mistakes as stepping stones for growth in Step 5.

Rejecting Old Stories Guided Meditation

1. Make yourself comfortable. Close your eyes if this feels comfortable for you and focus on your breath. As you focus on your breath, breathe deeply and slowly. Stay like this for a few moments until you enter a deep state of relaxation.

2. As you breathe in, silently say, 'I reject my old stories.' As you breathe out, think, 'I let go of these old stories.' Repeat this affirmation with each breath, letting it sink deeper into your consciousness.

3. Now, reflect on the stories from your past that may have shaped your perception of the world and yourself. Acknowledge how these narratives have influenced your view of yourself and what you're capable of or how life should be. As you become more aware of these stories, observe them without judgment as if watching them from the outside, like on a TV screen.

4. Acknowledge these stories' impact on your life choices and relationships. But know that these stories are the ones that hold you back, the ones that stop you from believing

in yourself, and the ones that tell you you're not capable. Recognize that these were just one way of viewing the world. Now that you're rejecting your old stories, you can see the world and yourself differently.

5. Visualize these old thoughts on pieces of paper. Now, imagine a gentle breeze blowing and watch as each piece is carried away, dissolving into the air, no longer part of your present reality. Feel the lightness as you release each story, experiencing the freedom from the restraints of the past.

6. With the old stories released, your mind is now open to more compassionate, creative, and expansive views of yourself and the world.

7. Imagine yourself nourishing these new perspectives each time you breathe in, helping them to grow and flourish. Repeat silently or aloud, whichever feels right for you, the following affirmations:

    - I am rejecting my old stories.
    - I am thinking more positively.
    - I am embracing challenges with confidence.

8. Take a few deep breaths and embrace these affirmations in your heart. When you feel ready, slowly bring your awareness back to the present moment and open your eyes if they were closed.

9. In your mind's eye, see yourself moving forward with confidence and clarity. You can break free from the past, reject your old stories, and achieve whatever your heart desires.

10. Take a moment to feel the lightness, freedom, and possibilities ahead. When you feel ready, carry this new mindset into your day.

Affirm:
I release my negative thoughts and embrace positivity.

BECOME YOUR AUTHENTIC SELF

Step 4

The fourth step is discovering and understanding who you are, as well as your values, desires, and beliefs.

Now that you have rejected your old stories and reframed your negative self-talk, you're ready to move on to the next part of the journey: becoming your authentic self.

We hear the word 'authenticity' bandied around so often these days. Since the rise of social media, it's become a popular topic of discussion. We often hear the advice to 'be authentic,' 'present our authentic selves,' 'stay true to ourselves,' and so on, but what exactly is true authenticity, and why is it essential in your self-esteem journey?

UNDERSTANDING AUTHENTICITY

In simple terms, authenticity is all about embracing who you really are. It means being yourself and being true to your values, desires, and beliefs – and it means operating from a place of genuineness. This can be incredibly challenging in a world that rewards conformity and where we are often driven to seek external validation. But when we live from our authentic selves and confidently express who we are and what we truly desire, the benefits unfurl, leading to a deeper sense of fulfillment, confidence, and purpose. The impact is transformative:

- You increase your chances of achieving what you want in life.
- You experience less internal conflict. Instead, you feel like you're living in alignment.

- You're more self-aware, and this enables you to make better decisions, whether that's a mundane day-to-day decision, such as what brand of tea to choose, or a major life decision, like choosing a partner.

- You have a clear vision of what you desire in life and in your relationships.

- You're able to assert a stronger sense of self-control.

- You understand your motivations and what does and doesn't serve you.

- Your values serve as your internal compass, guiding you to a deeper knowing and providing direction in life.

Authenticity strengthens self-esteem, because it helps you to cultivate genuine connections. It enhances your mental health, increases fulfillment, reduces stress and anxiety, and, overall, helps you foster a stronger sense of purpose.

When we're authentic, we're the unsuppressed versions of ourselves. We can truly learn to embrace our unique qualities and appreciate who we are as individual creations on this earth. Your authentic self is the core of who you are – the most genuine version of yourself – and authentic living is critical to personal growth and fulfillment, and can lead you to your higher self.

However, when people experience low self-esteem they often lose a sense of who they are, because they try to conform to what they think others want to see within them. For so many years, I battled with who my authentic self was and I showed up with different identities depending on the groups of people I was around. To some extent, we all have different personas, and it can be part of being emotionally intelligent when we can adjust to our social circumstances and communicate with people in a way that feels fitting to that group. We have many facets to our personalities and different elements of who we are, and just because different parts of you come out with different people doesn't mean you're fake. In our lives, we often navigate various social circles where we embody different personas. We can still be in alignment with our core values, genuine spirit, soul and beliefs, but we share different parts of ourselves at different times. For instance, we portray our professional selves at work, but, with old friends from school, we may lean into a more nostalgic version of ourselves. However, the difference between authenticity and not being your true self lies in maintaining constant alignment with your inner values and individual identity. For example, if you're willing to go along with things you don't really believe in just to fit in, this isn't authenticity. However, if you're willing to accept others' views but can challenge issues that aren't aligned with your core values, this is an act from your authentic self – your higher self. Staying grounded in our core values remains crucial, as they guide us in remaining true to ourselves across our diverse identities.

The journey to embracing my true self was gradual, spanning many years of introspection and personal growth. I delved deep into my inner work and a pivotal moment arrived when I embarked on the entrepreneurial path, as launching your own business presents challenges that push you in every direction imaginable. From the fear of leaving the security of employment to asking myself, 'Will I be able to pay my mortgage and feed my children?' every fear I experienced took some digging deep into my soul to trust in myself and make my dream possible. My dream is to have freedom from the constraints of employment, to be able to take and pick up my children to and from school without having to compromise my mornings by dropping them off at someone else's house at 6:30 a.m., and to have as many holidays in the year as I want without having to ask permission from someone else. This, to me, will give me the most enormous sense of authenticity. The chaotic yet cherished moments of Sunday dinners with my extended family, filled with laughter and the bustling energy of children, nieces, and nephews, alongside the joyous holiday escapades with my husband and daughters – these collective experiences shape the essence of who I am. As I grow, each moment propels me closer to embracing my authentic self.

THE JOURNEY TO YOUR AUTHENTIC SELF

Self-discovery is an ongoing process that paves the way to embracing your authenticity. I encourage you to be excited about this journey and remember that it's a continuing process of evolution. Know that we're all on this same journey, with vulnerabilities and areas for growth – it's part of our human experience.

Your authentic self will likely evolve through the ages and stages of life. When you tap into your soul and nurture the parts of you that need to be nurtured, you can fully embrace who you are. There is no better reward than to gain this deeper connection and understanding of who you are. Your authentic self is the unapologetic version of yourself just as you are, and by that, I don't mean not apologizing for your mistakes; I mean becoming a person who knows precisely what their needs, desires, and passions are – somebody who doesn't rely on the opinions of others, but serenely and confidently knows exactly who they are and what they bring to the world. Your authentic self doesn't need to strive and boast about your accolades. They have a deep and confident connection with them.

It's time to step forward into the most authentic version of you – and it starts with being clear on your values.

Uncover Your Personal Values

Acknowledging your values helps you determine what makes a successful and meaningful life; they're your personal measure of fulfillment and joy. When you have a firm conviction of what you care about and, more importantly, what not to care about, you learn to let go of the things that don't matter to you. In return, you build resilience and create more happiness and freedom in your life. A deeper understanding of your identity can help you feel happier, experience less inner conflict, and harness the ability to say no to those things you don't feel aligned with. One of the foundations of strong self-esteem is knowing your own mind and being able to express this.

Understanding the values you stand for can help you make better decisions and underpin your motivations for achieving the goals you desire to work toward. Research has shown that just thinking or writing about our values can make us more likely to take inspired action toward our goals.[12] Motivating people with their underpinning values can keep them going even in the face of adversity. So, clarify your values to get you closer to achieving your goals.

There is a tool called VITALS that has been developed by Meg Selig to help you cultivate your sense of self and strengthen your identity. VITALS helps us acknowledge the different factors to consider when fostering deeper self-awareness: values, interests, temperaments, activities, life mission, and strengths. I encourage my clients to examine their VITALS and understand what drives them. In this

---

12 Selig, M. (2016). 'Know Yourself? 6 Specific Ways to Know Who You Are,' *Psychology Today*: www.psychologytoday.com/gb/blog/changepower/201603/know-yourself-6-specific-ways-to-know-who-you-are? [Accessed March 11, 2025]

exercise, developed by Selig, you will get to understand what your VITALS are, too.[13]

VITALS

Part 1: What Are Your Values?

Please take a moment to reflect on what your values are. Here are a few examples. I encourage you to add your own:

- **Integrity:** upholding honesty, ethics, and moral principles
- **Compassion:** showing empathy and kindness toward others
- **Respect:** valuing others' opinions, beliefs, and boundaries
- **Gratitude:** appreciating the good in one's life and expressing thanks
- **Creativity:** valuing innovation, originality, and imagination
- **Curiosity:** seeking knowledge, learning, and understanding
- **Responsibility:** taking ownership of one's actions and obligations
- **Belief in a higher power:** a belief that there exists a force, entity, or deity that transcends the physical world
- **Being a reliable friend:** prioritizing your friendships
- **Being a supportive partner:** being caring, supportive, and loving in your relationships

Part 2: What Are Your interests?

Interests form a considerable part of our identity.

---

13 Ibid.

From my journey, I know that a big part of developing authenticity was about embracing the things I enjoyed doing and ensuring I gave myself time to do them. For me, this is exercise, cooking, and writing.

Many of my clients who struggle with low self-esteem don't give themselves time to invest in their interests, hobbies, and passions. Often, this stems from feelings of not being worthy of investing time in themselves. To them, it feels too indulgent.

If this is you, I encourage you to prioritize your interests – it's a key part of your self-esteem journey. If you don't really know what your interests are, reflecting on these questions can be particularly helpful:

1. What do you enjoy doing?
2. What topics or interests are important to you?
3. How does it make you feel when you do these activities?

Part 3: What Is Your Temperament?

What are your natural preferences? Are you an extrovert who likes to spend time with groups of people, or are you more introverted and prefer spending time one-on-one? Maybe you're an easy-going, chill person, or an energetic, busy bee like me.

Embrace your qualities and learn who you are and what you prefer. Having more awareness of these things can help build your confidence, because it can help you understand where you can flourish and avoid situations that don't serve you.

Write down what your natural preferences are.

Part 4: What Are Your Around-the-Clock Activities?

The next step is to become aware of when you like to do things — your natural biorhythms. For example, are you a morning person, like me, or a night owl?

I love my sleep, so I'm always in bed early. If I stay up late, I feel grouchy the next day. I like to exercise in the morning, and I'm more productive in the morning than in the evening.

These biorhythms help us identify when we're at our most productive and when we need to rest. It can help us schedule activities when we're at our best and respect our innate biology. This is all part of knowing yourself better and forming that stronger authenticity.

Write down what your own natural biorhythms are.

Part 5: What Is Your Life Mission?

One commonality I've observed during my career is the link between people having meaning and purpose in life and the levels of life satisfaction they experience. I've worked with people who get paid well and have secure and comfortable jobs, but who have no real sense of purpose, leading to a lack of fulfillment.

As I mentioned in an earlier chapter, when I started my journey toward my life purpose, I was working in a secondary school. I knew that job wasn't my lifelong mission, but what was helpful about this role was my realization of how much I enjoyed solving problems, helping people, and engaging with them. From then on, when I saw people come into school to provide therapy and support, I knew in my heart that I was destined to work in a caring profession. This led to me training as a social worker and then a therapist. I can honestly say that being a therapist is by far the most rewarding job I have ever had. Since realizing my purpose, I have built a successful, fulfilling business, done things I would never have dreamed of doing, appeared on the radio and

TV, and am now writing this book. These are the opportunities that I discovered by just listening to that inner voice tugging and pulling inside.

Reflect for a moment on the most meaningful encounters you have had in life. Describe what these experiences and encounters were. How do these experiences link to your life purpose?

Part 6: What Are Your Strengths?

Strengths include your abilities, skills, talents, and character traits, such as loyalty, emotional intelligence, patience, ambition, and so on. Knowing what your strengths are is the cornerstone of building good self-esteem.

Many people with low self-esteem find it difficult to acknowledge that they have any strengths, and they seldom praise themselves. But they're swift to berate themselves or point out their flaws. If you aren't used to focusing on your strengths, you'll likely experience some resistance here. It may feel unnatural for you to do this, but it's a game changer. Shift your focus from your perceived failures and weaknesses to your strengths and accomplishments.

We all possess some strengths, even if we don't have some amazing talent. It may be as simple as acknowledging your character strengths or realizing the qualities others see in you. Even if you are uncomfortable identifying your strengths, give this a try. For example, 'I am a good friend/determined/creative.'

If you find it hard to know your strengths, I encourage you to ask those you feel comfortable with, like family or friends, what strengths they see in you. Take a moment to create a text or copy this one I've created and send it to at least three people you trust:

> I'm currently reading a book, and one of the exercises it has asked me to do is text people I know and trust and ask them what they think my strengths/positive attributes are. So please may I ask you to let me know what you feel my strengths/positives are? Thank you.

When they have provided feedback, journal how this made you feel.

I hope this VITALS exercise has been helpful. What have you learned about yourself? Anything new? Or maybe it has helped consolidate some aspects of your character you already knew about.

I love this exercise as it helps us reflect on our unique qualities and realize that there's nothing wrong with having differences between us; this is a part of healthy self-esteem. We all have different personalities and we should embrace more of who we are and be more compassionate toward ourselves.

••••••••••••••••••

Align Your Actions with Your Values

If you ever feel that your life isn't fully aligned with your authentic self, remember that you have the power to make changes.

Your relationship with yourself is at the core of living authentically; it's about getting honest and open with yourself. Aligning your actions with your values and beliefs requires you to reflect on situations when they arise, whether in work, friendships, relationships, or any other problem you're dealing with, connecting with your authentic essence, and asking if these things align with your values.

For example, if you're in a relationship or friendship that you know doesn't align with your values, but you keep maintaining it, get honest with yourself and, as scary as it can feel, LISTEN to that inner voice! I've experienced this myself. I knew my values didn't align with my partner's anymore (maybe they never did in the first place), but it took me years to figure this out. When we stay in these situations, we compromise our authentic selves, effectively giving them the finger by ignoring that inner voice and our spirit and soul.

Check in with yourself when you're doing something and ask yourself: Am I genuinely interested in said activity or am I doing it because I think I should, or because it's what I think others expect of me? Does the situation match my own way of working, personality, and strengths? Does it make me feel happy, content, or, on the contrary, resentful, anxious, or uncomfortable? You can apply this to all areas of your life, from relationships to career/business.

Take note of your bodily responses. Do you feel nervous or on edge? Do you feel calm and collected? Our physical reactions are a great indication of whether we're living in alignment or despair.

The more you can do this, the more authentic your life will be and the more you'll tap into the story you want to tell about your life.

You only get one life and it's precious; you deserve to live a life that makes you happy and filled with abundance and endless possibilities. When we strengthen our esteem, we let go of conformity and listen to our true essence.

Let Go of What Others Think

When we experience low self-esteem, we can't fully embrace who we are and instead seek approval from external sources. As we'll come to see, this is a natural part of being human; we all do this in some capacity. However, it becomes a bigger issue when we live our lives pursuing acceptance from others. This restricts our ability to live truly from our authentic divine selves.

In Steps 1 and 2, we explored how past experiences, trauma, and social conditioning can hinder our ability to show up as our authentic selves. We fear that people will dislike us or won't accept us as we are. For individuals who have long sought love and acceptance from others and been rejected in some way through bullying, family rejection, or abuse, it can be an immensely intimidating challenge. Our human design, through evolution, means we were born to survive in groups. In the era of hunter-gatherers, mutual reliance was crucial for survival. This historical context helps us grasp why acceptance has become integral to our ability to navigate the world effectively. Of course, now we don't need to worry so much about this in terms of our survival. We understand that our lives don't depend on the approval of every individual, yet this knowledge aids us in comprehending the subconscious forces at work.

I used to care so much about what others thought of me; however, when I developed better self-esteem, I started to let go of that. I realized that other people would always have a view or an opinion of me. It may be good, bad, or neutral, but I had no control over what others thought. It became increasingly important that what I thought of myself mattered more. Over the past couple of years, I had an encounter where a fellow therapist sent me a text message outlining their opinions of something I'd posted on social media. In this post,

I shared some insights into attachment styles. I didn't ask this fellow therapist for her opinion, but she took it upon herself to express what she thought was incorrect about the post. When I reread my post and her opinion, she had clearly misinterpreted something. So, I messaged her back and pointed this out to her, which she then accepted and could see where I was coming from. However, this experience really rattled my confidence. I didn't express anger or become rude to her, but I asserted myself because I disagreed with her viewpoint. The sad fact is that she unfollowed me on Instagram, which really hurt me. I found it triggering because it felt like rejection, just like my experiences of being bullied in my teens. It showed me that my wounded and rejected inner child remained vulnerable to activation. I contemplated unfollowing her, but decided to rise above this, as I felt it was a childish act anyway and that I would choose to respond with love rather than anger. I am sharing this experience because it can take time to practice letting go of what others think – it's not an overnight process – but when you embrace freedom by breaking away from the confines of living by others' standards, judgments, and expectations, this is when life truly becomes liberating.

Of course, as we explored in Step 2, our perception of what other people think about us may be far from the truth – it's often down to our negative perceptions of what we think others may think of us. If I continued to hold on to what others think, I can tell you that you wouldn't be reading this book; my fear would have stopped me in my tracks. I have reached a point in my self-esteem journey where I really and truly don't care what anybody thinks of me. If I couldn't overcome this fear of what others thought about me, it would have stopped me in many areas of my life, like growing my business.

You may have also hidden parts of yourself from the world or conformed to social norms because you have felt that you wanted to match up to others' expectations. It's normal to want to be accepted by people – from a young age, we observe other children and we want to fit in; it's hard-wired into us to want to be liked and accepted by others. As adults, we continue to mimic the patterns from childhood, and we may subtly alter our behavior in the way we speak or show up in the world. We touched on this earlier and it's linked to emotional intelligence, which is being able to adjust your way of being in different social situations to help you connect with others. The danger comes when we don't have a strong sense of who we are and we let others dictate who we think we should be. Having good levels of esteem means we can stand firm in our values, morals, and who we are as individuals. To help you break free from the masks you wear, you need to shift the way you view differences between us. When you start to embrace your true self and others' uniqueness, it becomes inevitable that the masks just start to drop away, as you have the confidence to just be you.

One of the areas I have had to work on over the past five years is how I show up online as my authentic self. Using social media once seemed so scary. I feared people would think I was big-headed, self-centered, and stupid. I had to fight a lot of resistance, which wasn't easy. As an entrepreneur, I've embraced social media as a tool to connect with others and get my message out into the world, so that I can help as many people as possible. Previously, I perceived social media as a reflection of my level of worth and popularity. The transition has been challenging. As I mentioned in Step 2, social media has sometimes triggered my low self-esteem, leading me to refrain from using it at times. For many of us, learning to be visible and sharing snippets of who we are online can feel highly vulnerable. But when you're growing an online business, it's an essential aspect of growth and reach. So it's been something I've had to embrace and get used to. Using my internal resources – the things I knew

I needed to help me find strength, safety, and self-confidence – I adopted compassion toward myself, which helped me realize that I don't need approval from others. I also knew I wasn't doing anything wrong if I was just being myself. If I showed up as my authentic self from a place of integrity and with a mission to educate, inspire, and help others, and if people had a problem with that, it was none of my concern because it was more about their issues than mine.

Remember, being out of our comfort zone is part of growth, and I know that many people in business grapple with the same issues I've explored. If you're holding back parts of yourself from the world because of fear, I ask you to step into your authentic self. Show up on a live, post a video of yourself, talk to your audience, and observe how you feel. The more you do this, the more you grow.

Now, sometimes you might not get the engagement you're hoping for; some of us may even encounter hostility or differing opinions. Social media can feel slow and demotivating when we experience a lack of engagement or resistance from others. But remember, social platforms are busy places, and it often isn't personal – it just is! You may want to consider asking a couple of supportive friends to engage with your posts to boost their visibility and give you confidence. Reconnecting with your 'why' and focusing on helping just one person can help you to remain motivated. Hopefully, you'll soon start to realize that it's OK to share and be vulnerable, and that you can do this in a way that feels aligned and authentic to who you are.

I encourage you to step beyond your comfort zone, even if it feels unfamiliar at first. It's time to express your truth, share your innermost thoughts, and embrace engagement with the world rather than withdrawing. Low self-esteem often prompts us to conceal our authentic selves. I remember the days when I fretted over the potential judgment of others, particularly when posting online. Negative, hurtful thoughts would replay in my mind, and I would imagine their reactions. But it's essential to break free from this cycle, prioritize your own authenticity and well-being, and show the world who you are. Don't ever do this to expect a million likes. Do it because you're growing and stepping into your higher power, where you aren't controlled by the ego but led by the heart – this will become natural the more your esteem develops.

When you evolve into a higher version of yourself, living through authenticity becomes an effortless exercise that transcends any other person's thoughts or opinions about you. You feel safe and content. Knowing your authentic self is a gift. How often do you consider yourself a genuine gift to this world? I think it's so powerful to reflect that there is nobody else like you. Even if you're a twin, you are still unique. You still have your unique fingerprint, personality, and temperament. Like everything in nature, you're a unique being, and we aren't separate from nature. We are nature, too. We have distinctive characteristics, strengths, and qualities. When we fully embrace who we are and what we came here to be, we can own it and become authentic.

Unapologetically You!

I encourage you to take a moment to sit and reflect on who your authentic self is. Write down the things that make you YOU. What traits do you have? What quirks and qualities do you have?

I'll go first:

> My authentic self is wearing my favorite cardigan, despite it looking bobbly, old, and worn. I indulge in eating pizza

until my stomach is full, exhibit a little goofy behavior, and attend the gym because I love how it makes me feel. I also watch reality TV – *The Real Housewives of Cheshire*, *Billie & Greg: The Family Diaries*, and *Ferne McCann: My Family & Me* (please don't judge me!). I listen to old-school garage, Tina Turner, and Madonna. I also read self-help books for my healing, and to help my clients. My goal is to become a millionaire, because I like money and the freedom it gives me. I may decide to eat a whole pack of Haribo unashamedly, drink too much wine (occasionally), or listen to meditations because I love guided meditations. I also write because I now feel capable despite my dyslexia. I am kind, loyal, caring, ambitious, dedicated, and sensitive. I am these things. This is me.

I share this with you because I want you to practice getting in touch with who you are, as your sense of self is important. Who is your authentic self? Focus on your strengths, and know that your unique quirks and qualities matter.

....

Set Healthy Boundaries

Setting boundaries is crucial for moving forward as the most authentic version of yourself, but I see so many people with low self-esteem struggle to set essential boundaries in their relationships, work, and life. Examples are when people agree to things they don't want to do. It can also involve working extra hours or going above and beyond to deliver extra things when they aren't required to. Part of becoming your authentic self involves realigning with your needs and desires, and stopping conforming to the perceived or actual demands that others place on you. This doesn't mean you can't help people or support loved ones in your life. Rather, it's about learning to prioritize your own needs, which can help you cultivate more energy, presence, and time to dedicate to loved ones. And sometimes, this does mean being selective about what you invest your energies in.

Learning to say 'no' to things that aren't in alignment with your own values is so important. This helps you to protect yourself and your energies and ensure that you are prioritizing the things that are most important to you.

Many of my clients find it difficult to start saying no and to establish boundaries in relationships where they previously didn't exist. Asking yourself questions such as why you're doing something can help you to decipher if you're doing it from a place of authenticity because you want to, or if it's because you feel an expectation to do something, or you're doing it for someone else. Practice tapping into how your body feels when you are going to say yes or no to something: Does it feel right, or do you feel anxious, nervous, and uncomfortable? Do a body scan, which involves slowly paying attention to your body, section by section, and noticing any physical sensations without judging them. It's important to mention here that sometimes being out of our comfort zone is necessary for our growth, but it has to feel in alignment with our values and not to please others.

Setting boundaries becomes crucial for personal growth and well-being in a world that frequently demands constant availability and self-sacrifice. By defining healthy limits, you can make room for self-care, foster meaningful relationships, and engage in your passions with greater focus and intention. You can do this by deciding what activities you want to say 'yes' to and what you want to say 'no' to, deciding what your non-negotiables are in your relationships, and making sure you prioritize time to look after your own well-being and engage in activities that you enjoy.

Amy's Story

Amy, a 30-year-old professional, sought therapy due to persistent feelings of emptiness and a lack of self-identity. As a child, she had experienced abandonment from her dad, who left her mum and family when Amy was three years old. Her dad didn't keep in consistent contact with her throughout her childhood. She remembers constantly feeling like she wasn't good enough because of this. The negative thoughts from childhood continued to haunt her into adult life. It took many years for her to tell her close friends and family that she was gay, and she described herself as continually adapting her behavior to fit others' expectations, as she wanted them to like her. However, this led to feelings of disconnectedness from her true self. Her core belief that she wasn't lovable saw her adapt her behaviors to please others.

During our initial sessions, Amy struggled to articulate her feelings, often deferring to what she believed others wanted her to say. She expressed fears of rejection and abandonment if she revealed her authentic thoughts and emotions. This pattern extended to her personal and professional life, where she often felt like an imposter despite her achievements.

We explored her emotional responses and her beliefs about not being lovable or likable. We used techniques such as cognitive restructuring, which we explored in the previous step (see *pages 76–81*), to challenge negative self-perceptions and enhance her self-awareness. Mindfulness exercises also helped her connect with her present experiences and emotions.

Initially, she found it challenging to confront her true feelings, fearing judgment or rejection. However, as we progressed, she became more comfortable expressing herself authentically and was able to uncover the underlying fears and insecurities that fueled her need to please others. She started to realize that the pattern of seeking validation was due to the relationship breakdown with her dad. She began rebuilding a sense of self-worth independent of others' opinions by exploring and validating her values. Journaling exercises and self-reflection activities like the ones outlined in this book facilitated her journey toward authenticity. Her increased self-confidence and self-awareness translated into healthier relationships and a more fulfilling personal and professional life.

By the end of therapy, she reported a significant shift in her sense of identity and self-worth. She no longer needed to conform to others' expectations and embraced her unique qualities and values. Her journey highlights the transformative power of inner work.

Practice Forgiveness

Fostering deep forgiveness is essential to healing and forms an integral part of authenticity. By working on forgiveness and building on the work you did in the previous step of starting to develop a compassionate relationship with yourself and others, you become more aligned with who you are and can build a more authentic relationship with yourself.

Forgiveness is a deliberate decision that can help us overcome anger, resentment, and retribution toward ourselves and others. People often find it easier to offer forgiveness toward others than themselves. I observe this in clients who ruminate about themselves, resulting in feelings of self-disdain and shame. This eats away at their joy, leaving them with little self-respect and keeping them in a self-perpetuating cycle of internal verbal abuse, which further impedes the relationship they have with themselves. We can't truly be authentic if we refuse to forgive and accept ourselves. It's necessary to help us drop the façade and be comfortable with who we really are.

I work with many clients who cannot forgive their past mistakes or perceived shortcomings. Self-judgment stops them from fully embracing who they are, including their flaws and the things that may not have gone how they feel they should have. Adopting a sense of self-compassion and kindness is essential. By doing this, we accept ourselves, our histories, and the things that ultimately make us into the authentic beings we are. When we don't forgive our past mistakes, we use these self-judgments against ourselves. This lack of acceptance is a barrier to achieving complete authenticity. When we genuinely forgive ourselves, we're saying it's OK. We accept that these parts of us are an essential aspect of who we are, and that this is a true reflection of our authenticity. The more we forge forgiveness and acceptance of our identity, the more our authenticity can emerge.

A helpful tool involves taking yourself through eight stages:[14]

1. **Identify:** Identify the event or behavior you don't feel happy with.

2. **Explore:** Explore your part. What was your responsibility and what wasn't your responsibility?

3. **Accept and experience remorse:** When you have connected with the parts that you were responsible for, allow yourself to feel any emotions attached. There may be emotions such

---

14 Cornish, M. A. and Wade, N. G. (2015), 'A Therapeutic Model of Self-forgiveness with Intervention Strategies for Counsellors,' *Journal of Counseling & Development*, 93: 96–104: doi.org/10.1002/j.1556-6676.2015.00185.x [Accessed July 30, 2025].

as guilt or shame that arise. Feel these emotions and show compassion toward yourself. Be kind to yourself like you would a friend.

4. **Notice thoughts and feelings:** If you're feeling guilt or shame, try to understand this in the context of this one unique event or behavior. Try to detach the actions from your character – just because you did something you feel ashamed of doesn't make you a bad person.

5. **Make amends:** If you did something to upset another person, try to make amends with them. If there are no amends to be made, ask yourself if you're being harsh or self-critical toward yourself.

6. **Recommit:** Reaffirm your values, reflect on what is important to you, and take this as an opportunity for personal growth.

7. **Nurture compassion:** Show compassion to yourself for your actions and try to understand why you acted the way you did. Speak to yourself as you would a friend, offering understanding and forgiveness.

8. **Let go:** Release any negative thoughts and feelings. Do these thoughts contribute to unhelpful thinking patterns and continue the cycle of bad thoughts toward yourself? Let them go.

Practice Makes Perfect Progress

As you practice becoming more authentic and realize how you want to show up in the world, embodying this can feel a little scary. Authenticity links closely to our perception of self-worth. So, this can feel a little alien until you feel truly aligned with who you are and have absolute confidence and assurance that you are enough. You need to believe this at a deep, subconscious level, and this can take a while to achieve. This is why doing practices such as guided meditations and positive affirmations and practicing being your authentic self are so important. Working at the deeper layers of your consciousness, you can unravel years of negative experiences and destructive thinking patterns.

Practice listening to your inner voice more often and ensure this aligns with your most authentic self. Be aware of when social conditioning and the opinions of friends or family obstruct your true desires. Be in tune with how you feel around different people. Are there situations that make you feel more empowered to be authentically yourself and others that make you want to retreat? Developing authenticity is an ongoing process of self-awareness that takes practice.

••••

As we conclude this step, I encourage you to tap into your authentic self, develop a deep relationship with yourself, and embrace the journey toward genuine authenticity. A powerful message that the late Dr. Wayne Dyer expressed was the notion that 'You can't be authentic unless you're following your bliss.'[15] What he meant by this is that when you aren't aligned in your daily activities – such as being stuck in a job that you hate or a relationship that brings no happiness, or any other circumstance you wish to apply this to – that stops you from tapping into the essence of authenticity, because you aren't even being authentic to yourself... Ouch, that hurts! It's no coincidence that I came across that message in his book *Happiness Is the Way* while writing this chapter on authenticity. I've experienced this in my life; I've been in situations I knew weren't right for my higher self. Something needs to change when you start to feel unease regularly in your life.

---

15   Dyer, W. (2019), *Happiness Is the Way*. Carlsbad, C.A.: Hay House Inc.

We often try to ignore those icky feelings because the fear of changing the situation is too hard, uncomfortable, and scary. When we live in these conditions, we halt our chances of self-development and stagnate. Sometimes, making decisions to take action for change can take a while, but the earlier you start acknowledging your soul calling, the sooner you can take that path to find genuine authenticity in everything you do. When we align with who we are, we feel a sense of happiness and contentment in everything we do. We know we're on the path we are meant to be on because life feels light and happy. Being who you genuinely are enriches your every day, fills you with vitality, and makes life more pleasurable to experience. So, embrace this continuous journey of self-acceptance and compassion, which demands patience, determination, and bravery. Surrounding yourself with a supportive community can greatly aid in this ongoing process. Join us at www.natashapagemsc.com to become part of a community of kindred spirits dedicated to fostering a profound self-connection.

This self-discovery forms the bedrock of self-acceptance, which is the focus of the next step. It's time to fully and deeply accept and love who you are.

THERAPEUTIC EXERCISES

Self-Compassion Exercise

I would like you to think about a situation where you didn't act from a place of real authenticity – for example, when engaging in an activity because it was what someone else wanted you to do, or saying yes to something you didn't really want to do. I would then like you to write a compassionate letter to yourself, acknowledging your struggles, validating your emotions, and offering comfort and encouragement as you would to a dear friend.

This exercise is all about treating yourself with kindness, understanding, and acceptance, especially during challenging times or when facing self-doubt. It fosters self-acceptance, resilience, and a nurturing relationship with yourself, which are essential to authenticity. I've included an example here for you:

> Dear Natasha,
>
> I know I haven't been true to myself, but I've been trying to keep others happy. I offered to bake 100 cakes for the school fair. However, this put a lot of stress on me and made me lose my temper with my daughter. Sometimes, I say yes to doing these things because I worry that people won't like me. I show kindness to myself for trying to help others, but I realize now that I try to do things to keep them happy so they will think I'm a nice person and want to be my friend. I also realize that it was too much for me to take on and that, because I work full-time in my job, I shouldn't have committed to making all of those cakes. I know now that I must start saying no and putting my needs first. Having boundaries and looking after my well-being is OK, and saying no doesn't make me a bad person.
>
> With love, Natasha x

Spending Time Alone

I would like you to spend at least an hour, if not more, on an activity that brings you joy and happiness or makes you feel good. This might be reading a book in peace on your own or taking yourself out for a coffee, or it could be booking a spa day on your own, listening to your favorite music and dancing around the house, or engaging in something creative like writing, art, or cooking.

Spending time alone allows you to connect with who you are, your passions, and your interests, helping you to build a stronger connection to your authentic self.

After this consciously planned time alone, take some time to reflect, journaling about how it made you feel.

Becoming Your Authentic Self Guided Meditation

1. Make yourself comfortable. Close your eyes if this feels comfortable for you and focus on your breath. As you focus on your breath, breathe deeply and slowly. Stay like this for a few moments until you enter a deep state of relaxation.

2. As you focus on your breath, consider the question 'Who am I really?' Without judgment, allow whatever thoughts and emotions that arise just to be. Know that your true self is a unique expression of love. You are an authentic gift to this world.

3. You are now connecting with your true self – the most authentic version of you. There is no need to hide or pretend who you are, because you are enough just as you are. Your authenticity is needed in this world.

4. Know that you are free to be exactly who you are. Let this truth set you free from the pretense and masks that you wear to fit in with other people. You are enough as you are; your authentic self is all you ever need to be.

5. Sitting with this awareness, imagine your authentic self and how it would feel and what it would look like in your daily life. How would you show up in the world when fully and

truly embracing your authentic self? Imagine yourself going about your daily tasks and interacting with people, feeling balanced and at peace, fully aligned and in harmony with who you are.

6. Please take a few moments to connect with this inner knowing and peace, and fully embrace how amazing it feels to show up as your true self.

7. Take a few more deep breaths, embedding this affirmation into your heart. When you feel ready, slowly bring your awareness back to the present moment. Open your eyes if they were closed, stretch if you want to, and continue your day. Carry the inner knowing that you are your authentic self, knowing that you are enough, just as you are.

·····················

Affirm:

I embrace who I am and who I want to be. I am authentically me.

DEVELOP YOUR SELF-ACCEPTANCE

Step 5

The fifth step involves embracing and being at peace with yourself, and adopting a more compassionate relationship with the self.

In the last step, you worked hard to uncover your authentic self, which is the foundation for self-acceptance. In this step, we'll be taking that practice deeper as you adopt a more positive sense of self and become more compassionate and loving toward yourself.

Over the years, I've observed how many of my clients with low self-esteem struggle with self-acceptance. Self-acceptance is indeed one of the most challenging steps to master – it's a process that takes deep inner work and healing; however, it's also one of the most rewarding. Self-acceptance is the key to a deeper and more personal relationship with the most crucial person in your life. Yes, that's YOU. It requires embracing and loving yourself unconditionally; a profound love that radiates to everyone around you. We can sense someone who loves themselves, and we can perceive someone who doesn't. When my clients start to love who they are, they're finally able to step into their higher power.

This step of self-acceptance begins with nurturing a genuine relationship with yourself, one where you embrace your true self without judgment. It means seeing yourself in a new way, recognizing your strengths and flaws, and choosing to love and accept yourself unconditionally. Adopting this unwavering positive regard creates a safe space within which self-compassion and understanding can flourish. This shift allows you to accept who you are, not just in your moments of jubilance, but also in times of vulnerability, fostering authentic self-love and inner harmony.

HOW THERAPEUTIC APPROACHES CAN HELP YOU DEVELOP SELF-ACCEPTANCE

My training as an integrative therapist has taught me many different theoretical approaches, but the one I'm most naturally drawn to work with is a person-centered approach. Founder Carl Rogers believed that, given the right conditions, a person can reach their full potential and become their true self – a term he called self-actualization.[16] In therapy, this involves the core conditions of:

- **Unconditional positive regard:** This is the way the therapist feels toward the client. They value them as an individual and accept them without judgment.

- **Congruence:** This is when the therapist is open and honest with the client. This may involve challenging the client to see things from a different angle, with respect and openness.

- **Empathic understanding:** This is when the therapist walks in the client's shoes – they really get in touch with how the client is experiencing the issues in their life.

When these core conditions are present in the relationship between the therapist and the client, this is where the magic happens and people can tune in to their intuition and understand what they need to change in order to move forward with more autonomy, confidence, self-acceptance, and love. This approach can teach us a lot about

---

16 Rogers, C. R. (1995; originally published 1961), *On Becoming a Person: A Therapist's View of Psychotherapy*. Boston: Houghton Mifflin, pp.187–196.

the power we all have within us if we adopt the core conditions and apply them to our relationship with ourselves.

You can learn unconditional positive regard and accept and value who you are, flaws and all. You can also develop congruence, which means being honest and transparent with yourself. And you can adopt empathy and understanding for yourself and ultimately develop self-compassion. This will enable you to treat yourself like your own best friend. These core conditions are so powerful in the journey to self-acceptance and, in this chapter, I have included exercises and tools to help you develop them.

EMBRACE ALL ASPECTS OF YOURSELF

In the realm of personal growth, terms such as self-acceptance, self-love, self-care, and compassion are frequently mentioned. But how do we truly cultivate and deeply feel love and acceptance for ourselves, especially when we have undergone experiences that have flawed our self-perception?

True self-acceptance begins with fostering unconditional positive regard. You have already gone some way toward this with the tools you've learned in the previous steps, such as challenging negative self-talk, focusing on your strengths, and letting go of what others think. But now it's time to really accept your innate attributes, whether positive or negative, without judgment. This can include body acceptance, self-protection from negative criticism, and believing in your capabilities.

As we've seen, low self-esteem stops us from fully accepting and embracing who we are, leading to us seeking validation from others. We seek approval from others rather than ask ourselves whether we approve of ourselves. True self-acceptance doesn't mean that you won't ever care again what people think of you, but it does mean that any actions, opinions, and negativity directed toward you from others will impact you less. A deeper understanding of yourself means you'll also have a deeper understanding of others. This will help you know that their judgments of you reflect their struggles, not yours. With this outlook, you'll find it much easier not to let others' opinions have a hold on you. You can let go of their opinions, and this is when self-acceptance is at its most powerful.

We often cling to messages that it's big-headed or boastful to love who you are. Thinking positively about yourself may feel especially uncomfortable when you experience low self-esteem, because the fear of rejection from others speaks louder than the voice within you. It can feel unsafe if you've had negative experiences of receiving praise. For example, a client I once worked with was academically very able, and she had been a naturally bright child. She recalled a time in her adolescence when the teacher praised her in front of the whole class for a piece of work she had done to a high standard. This led to some of her peers making fun of her. This experience taught her that having the gifts she had been given wasn't safe. After this incident, she often downplayed her abilities and didn't want to contribute as much in class. This example helps us to realize that embracing your uniqueness is about embracing every aspect of your being.

A helpful place to start is to go back to the VITALS exercise you did in Step 4 (*see pages 100–104*) and remind yourself of the strengths you identified. Every being on this planet has extraordinary and unique qualities. Even if you don't feel they're anything special, I can assure you that your unique qualities will bring something valuable to the world. It could seem so mundane or normal to you, but someone in your life will appreciate your qualities even if you haven't fully embraced them yourself. Think about some things you do in your life that make others happy. Are you a great cook, for example? Do you make wonderful cakes or entertain others? Are you good at a craft or hobby? Or maybe you like to write, sing, dance, and so on... You might have unique physical qualities, such as tight, curly hair and auburn-colored locks. Are you tall or small? Whoever or whatever you are, YOU ARE UNIQUE.

Often, I observe how people with low self-esteem shy away from sharing their unique gifts and talents. They may feel like they aren't good enough at something or haven't reached a certain level to feel confident enough to share with anyone else. Societal norms, peer pressure, and self-doubt can be the biggest barriers to people sharing their unique talents with the world. But our differences matter, because they contribute not only to our fulfillment when we tap into our passions and purpose in life, but also to the richness of society. So allow yourself to express your thoughts and emotions without fear of judgment. This process of self-exploration and self-acceptance can lead to greater clarity, self-understanding, and personal growth. I encourage you to adopt this type of relationship with yourself.

Self-acceptance is no easy feat; it's so hard to break free from the negative chatter. But one thing that can help us to alleviate our distress is remembering that nobody – yep, absolutely nobody – is perfect on this Earth. It can help to lessen the blow when we realize that we aren't meant to be perfect. Try viewing things you perceive as flaws with a little more love. When you have thoughts of 'I'm not enough,' catch yourself and tell yourself that you are enough just as you are, even with your imperfections.

Use your self-awareness as a tool to acknowledge the things you find challenging or to reflect when you make a mistake. Instead of criticizing yourself, though, see these things as little indications that this is an area for growth. Instead of feeling crappy, reflect on how you can learn from the scenario and know deep inside that there will be a purpose – a reason – for the lesson you're being taught. When we can see our mistakes as stepping stones for growth, it feels so much more inspiring than using them as a justification for our inadequacy.

One of my own experiences was failing my driving test. I didn't just fail once; I failed over and over again. After each experience of failing, I was naturally disappointed, but I used the experiences to help me grow. I realized I wasn't as good at maneuvers as I needed to be and I also realized one of the contributing factors was my anxiety: My huge desire to pass made me anxious on the day of the test. These 'failings' helped me to realize how important it was for me to pass my driving test. And it also helped me to recognize my determination and willingness to never give up! I did pass in the end – I was eight months pregnant at the time with my first daughter and it was such an incredible feeling to get that pass!

Some Tips for Redefining a Failure or Mistake

- Use failure as confirmation that you need to learn something.

- Don't define yourself by the mistake – just because you made a mistake, it doesn't mean you're not good enough; it just means you have some improvements to make.

- See it as an opportunity to grow resilience and bounce back stronger or approach things in a different way than the original plan.

••••

When you learn how to truly accept yourself and see your mistakes as areas for growth, you can overcome barriers to self-acceptance and let go even more of the identities you developed based on your past experiences and conditioning. As we explored in Step 3, CBT can help us create a level of awareness where we can change our thought processes toward ourselves and tune in to who we really are and what we truly desire. Engaging in mindfulness practices, seeking mentorship or coaching, journaling, participating in support groups, and exploring creative outlets are additional ways to foster personal growth and self-awareness. The exercises in this step will also support you with this.

Jasvinder's Story

Jasvinder, 39, posted some content online about her ex-boyfriend. In the posts, she called him names and shared details of some of the issues she was unhappy with in the relationship. Days after she had posted them, her ex made contact with her – he was furious because his mum had seen the messages. A few days on, once she had calmed down, Jasvinder realized that she had made a mistake. She felt bad about herself, but then managed to use her self-awareness by exploring this more deeply. She realized that she was seeking external validation through the likes and comments, and that this was to make her feel worthy. When she understood this, she knew this was something she could embrace and learn from, and that she needed to work on her own insecurities rather than seek approval from others. She made amends, removed the post, and apologized to her ex-partner.

When We Don't Like Who We Are

Many of us find it difficult to embrace certain aspects of ourselves if we aren't yet in a place of self-alignment – and sometimes there may be aspects we hold shame around. For example, I've supported some clients who struggle with issues such as regulating their emotions; they fly off the handle quickly or react to situations in ways they know are disproportionate to the problem. Hands up, this has been something I've also experienced, and it can make you feel so much shame when you say or do things to the people you love in anger or hurt. At the heart of these reactions is often low self-esteem. As we saw in Step 1, for some, this has been their coping mechanism – putting up their emotional defenses is often the result of what they were role-modeled in childhood or is based in traumatic experiences.

It can be painful to realize that we may not like aspects of our character, but I encourage you to see this as a positive insight, as this is where the work begins. When we realize that there are aspects of ourselves we don't like, this is a positive step forward, for it is only when we start to identify those character traits that we aren't happy with that we can begin to work on them. And rest assured that many of us feel this way. Trust me, I've worked with hundreds of people and this is something that comes up for so many.

Loving and accepting who you are can be transformative. There are aspects of ourselves that we cannot change, and embracing and loving all of who we are is essential. I believe in encouraging self-acceptance rather than urging people to alter themselves. Over time, this acceptance fosters genuine self-love.

Shadow Work

Shadow work, a concept developed by the renowned psychoanalyst Dr. Carl Jung, is a powerful form of psychotherapy. It delves into the often-hidden parts of our psyche, such as resentment and trauma, which we tend to repress or deny. This 'shadow self' is brought to the forefront in shadow work, offering a transformative journey toward increased self-awareness, emotional healing, and enhanced self-esteem.

Jung believed that we all have a persona, which is the personality we display to the public. The shadow self is the aspect of us that we keep hidden. Unlike the persona, the shadow self often includes traits that a person doesn't like to show. Jung didn't view this aspect as a negative, but as an essential part of our psyche. Shadow work, in its essence, is a non-judgmental exploration of our hidden aspects, helping us manage impulses we usually ignore. Our shadow self is a result of our social conditioning through distressing or traumatic experiences.

There is a short exercise at the end of this step that provides an opportunity for you to practice shadow work on your own (*see pages 149–151*). Techniques like shadow work can help us foster self-acceptance and adopt a more loving relationship with ourselves. When we can accept the parts of ourselves that we may not necessarily like, we foster a new acceptance of our imperfections. When we overcome the shame we may hold around these elements of ourselves we don't like, it becomes easier for us to treat ourselves with more love and kindness. We learn to love ourselves despite these parts of us.

Isaac's Story

Isaac, 29, struggled with social anxiety for most of his life, particularly concerning his appearance. He has a prominent birthmark on his face that he has always been self-conscious about. As a child, he was teased and often felt different, which led to him avoiding situations.

When Isaac first came to see me, he was in a bad place; he felt frustrated and was low in mood. He felt like his birthmark defined him in the eyes of others and that it was the first thing people noticed about him. He often avoided looking in mirrors or talking to new people.

We explored how his childhood experiences had shaped his perception of himself and the world. I helped him by normalizing his wanting to be accepted by others and explained that many people worry about their appearance. However, I started to help him realize the importance of distinguishing between how others perceive us and how we perceive ourselves.

We completed therapeutic exercises such as reframing how he saw his birthmark – not as a flaw, but as a unique feature contributing to who he was. I encouraged him to complete mindfulness and self-acceptance meditations, and to practice looking at himself in the mirror and acknowledging his birthmark without judgment. This process was very difficult for him at first, but, over time, he began to feel less distress when he looked in the mirror.

We also started to identify people in his life who loved him. Isaac realized that they didn't care about his birthmark; they loved him for his kindness, creativity, and humor. This realization was eye-opening for him and allowed him to start seeing himself from the perspective of those who cared about him.

As therapy progressed, he began challenging himself by slowly stepping out of his comfort zone. He attended some social events and started to practice positive self-talk. Though he still felt some waves of anxiety, he was learning to cope with it instead of letting it control him. We worked on self-acceptance and the importance of recognizing that some things, like his birthmark, were beyond his control and that they didn't diminish his value as a person.

Toward the end of his therapy journey, he shared that he had begun to see his birthmark as a symbol of resilience. It was part of his story, and while it might not be something he loved, it no longer negatively defined him. He even began to appreciate the conversations it sparked and how it allowed him to connect with others with visible differences.

DEVELOP SELF-COMPASSION

The next step in developing self-acceptance is self-compassion. Paul Gilbert developed the practice of compassion-focused therapy (CFT), as he believes the key is not to focus solely on self-esteem but to use self-compassion, because its emphasis is on how we treat ourselves when things go badly.[17]

Using CFT techniques is another valuable therapeutic tool that can significantly help heal those of us who struggle with shame and self-criticism. As we have already explored, many clients I work with experience feelings of shame, often because of their past experiences from issues such as abuse or neglect, breakdown in relationships, or just life in general. Some of the many negative messages we take on from others throughout our life's journey – such as through bullying or negative comments from our peers, or experiences of how family

---

17 Gilbert, P. (2010), *The Compassionate Mind (Compassion Focussed Therapy)*. London: Constable.

members have treated us – become imprinted on our hearts. As a result, the psyche and unconscious mind can become hardwired to feel deep levels of shame and self-loathing. At a conscious level, we become attuned to how others view us and worry that we aren't good enough.

Showing self-compassion means we care for ourselves and demonstrate compassion and understanding toward ourselves, just as we would toward a friend or family member. Building this new relationship with the self is the route to cultivating the conditions that nurture true self-esteem – the esteem that has you knowing you're the most important person you'll ever have a relationship with. Befriending yourself is the key to laying the groundwork for this relationship.

CFT techniques nurture self-compassion, with Gilbert's research showing that they effectively regulate our mood. This leads to feelings of safety, comfort, and self-acceptance – our ultimate goal. CFT helps us to grasp the science of the mind–body connection and promotes practices that enhance our body awareness. For more in-depth information about CFT and its benefits, I encourage you to refer to Paul Gilbert's work – he is a pioneer in the industry. Here, I share some of the techniques he recommends for developing more self-compassion.

Guided Imagery

Guided imagery helps people visualize their ideal compassionate selves. First, reflect on what you want to gain from completing a guided imagery. For example, is it to increase self-love, or to improve confidence, or some kind of emotional healing? Get yourself into a relaxed and comfortable place. You may want to ask someone to read a guided imagery script to you or find one on an app or online. A useful tip can be to record the scripts in your own voice.

As mentioned earlier, there's something powerful about hearing your own voice speaking them to you.

Guided imagery is something I often use in sessions with my clients. I use a calm and slow-paced voice to lead them into the imagery. I also recommend practicing slow, deep breathing to settle the body and mind, and encourage you to do the same. The meditations at the end of each step can be used to facilitate a guided imagery experience. Meditation involves focusing attention and awareness to achieve a calm yet heightened sense of awareness and presence, while specific guided imagery can be used as a way to facilitate this experience through following a script or listening to a recorded version of one.

Soothing Rhythm Breathing

Soothing rhythm breathing (SRB) involves slow, deep breathing with an even rhythm. This type of breathing activates the parasympathetic nervous system, which helps to calm the mind and body and regulate your emotions, allowing you to create a sense of safety, thus promoting relaxation and reducing anxiety. It helps develop self-compassion by shifting your emotional state from stress or self-criticism to a sense of kindness, warmth, and self-acceptance.

Practicing SRB

1. Find a comfortable position.
2. Start by breathing steadily and rhythmically in and out for four to five seconds. Inhale and exhale slowly and deeply.

3. Now, inhale through your nose for five to six seconds and exhale through your mouth for five to six seconds, allowing any tension to release.

4. Maintain a gentle and soothing pace using a rhythmic breathing pattern and tapping into your body and its senses.

5. As you breathe, imagine a sense of warmth, comfort, or safety spreading through your body.

6. Repeat this cycle four times, or more if you wish.

Compassionate Letter Writing

Another tool we can use to help us become more compassionate is letter writing. Gilbert's research shows that it can be helpful to express our emotions by writing things down.

Writing a Self-Compassion Letter

For this exercise, you will need to find a quiet, comfortable space.

Think of a situation that you struggled with in the past, or that you're struggling with now. While writing this letter, imagine you're speaking to a dear friend who is going through what you experienced or are experiencing. Offer yourself kindness, understanding, and encouragement.

When I first submitted my book proposal to write this very book you are now reading, I wasn't successful in gaining a book deal. I was so disappointed – I cried and felt like a failure. I've included an example of a self-compassion letter here for you, based on this experience:

Dear Natasha,

I know you're feeling disappointed because you didn't get offered a book deal immediately. It would be best if you tried to realize how far you have come by even submitting the book proposal. That is something many people never manage to complete.

You have been thinking negatively – that you're stupid and not good enough. However, that is not the truth. Just because you were unsuccessful this time, it doesn't define who you are. You are not stupid; you are brave and dedicated to this process. Now that you have had the chance to reflect on the book proposal, maybe some things could be improved, which is OK. It's often part of the process and can help improve the book.

You are talented, dedicated, and capable of amazing things. This setback is just a stepping stone to the journey, not the end of it. Take this time to reflect on how far you've come and believe there will be a better outcome.

With love, Natasha x

Now it's your turn.

How did you feel about writing this letter and consciously being kind and caring toward yourself? Can you try to talk to yourself more often from this compassionate and kind perspective?

•••••••••••••••••••

Compassionate Self-Talk

Over the years, I've seen how unfavorably some of my clients talk to themselves. Honestly, they say some terrible things to themselves, such as how stupid they are, how bad they feel for letting others down, or how much they hate aspects of themselves. As we've explored in earlier steps, the words we speak to ourselves matter. They form the basis of our relationship with the self.

Observe how you treat others compassionately and reflect on your compassion toward the people you care about. For example, if a friend or family member made a mistake, how would you try to comfort them? What kind of words would you say to them? The aim of adopting compassion toward yourself is to treat yourself in the same way. By becoming more aware of how you show compassion to others, you can adopt these ways of being in your relationship with yourself.

Would you tell your best friend they weren't good enough? Would you tell them that they're a failure or that they're unlovable? I certainly hope not. But you see, many of us easily fall into this dialogue through the inner chat we have with ourselves, and this prevents us from embracing our imperfections. Yet, as we explored earlier, it's these very flaws that make us unique and lovable. Try replacing self-criticism with self-compassion and allowing yourself to be the imperfect human you are. We are all imperfect! We get things wrong, make mistakes, say stupid things, do stupid things, and look uncool. But when we adopt self-compassion, we don't beat ourselves up. We embrace our flaws and sometimes can even learn to laugh at ourselves.

Talking to ourselves with compassion is much the same as letter writing. We learn to practice compassionate self-talk, which involves replacing harsh, judgmental inner dialogue with compassionate, gentle words and tones. We learned the principles of reframing negative self-talk in Step 3 (*see pages 77–78*), which is a pivotal factor in self-compassion. It involves shifting how we talk to ourselves; for example, replacing 'I'm such a failure' with 'I'm struggling right now, and that's OK – everyone struggles sometimes.' Similarly, self-compassion focuses on adopting a caring attitude in the way we talk to ourselves, but with more emphasis on really showing love and care toward ourselves, which goes deeper than the simple reframing of thoughts. We demonstrate love, empathy, and care toward ourselves.

Some of you may feel that self-compassion is selfish and indulgent. You may have concerns that it'll harm how people view you when you look after yourself more. To overcome this, it's helpful to start recognizing when you're being self-critical by pausing and noticing any self-judgmental thoughts. The following exercise will help you to compassionately interrupt the negative feedback loop.

Taking a Two-Minute Self-Compassion Break

I encourage you to practice self-compassion when self-critical thoughts arise in the moment.

1. **Pause:** When you notice a self-critical thought, pause briefly, close your eyes if this feels comfortable for you, and take a deep breath.
2. **Acknowledge:** Recognize that feeling unworthy is difficult; it makes us uncomfortable and distressed.
3. **Reframe:** Now practice saying something kind to yourself, like, 'I'm doing the best I can, and that's enough.'
4. **Visualize:** Spend a few seconds picturing a small, positive step you'll take next to move forward, no matter how minor that step might appear.

These are some of the core CFT techniques that will help you to build a more compassionate relationship with the self, helping you to manage difficult emotions, reduce self-criticism, and promote emotional well-being.

....

Integrate Self-Compassion into Your Daily Life

You can integrate self-compassion into your everyday life by having daily check-ins with yourself. Just like when we ask someone we care about if they're OK, self-compassion allows us time to reflect on our feelings and offer warmth and understanding as and when needed. For example, when I've spent the whole day working with my therapy clients, I may feel emotionally drained, like I need to have some quiet time alone. When I'm not being compassionate to myself, I ignore my own needs, continuing with tasks such as rushing my children to their after-school clubs, cooking the evening meal, doing other household chores, and so on, until I feel burned out. However, when I demonstrate self-compassion, I tap into what I need. This may be sitting down and having a cuppa, delegating who cooks the dinner that evening, or asking the kids to take a week off their clubs so that I don't have to be responsible for the drop-off and pick-ups that week, thereby preserving some of my energy.

Another way we can incorporate self-compassion into our lives is by building small gestures into our everyday routines. For me, this is through rituals such as my daily guided meditations before bed. As a therapist, business owner, mother, and wife, I often give a lot of compassion and emotional energy to others. This means it's important for me to adopt self-compassion and care for myself, so that I can support the people I work with and my family.

Think about how you could weave self-compassion into your day-to-day life. The exercise on pages 145–146 will take this further and help you to incorporate mindful 'me time' into your day.

Self-compassion is a powerful tool for emotional health and resilience. I urge you to learn to be kind to yourself, especially when you face challenges or setbacks. This is normal and, trust me, I know from my own experience and those I support that it's part of the journey. Like many of the practices we've explored so far, self-compassion requires a commitment; it's an ongoing process rather than a one-off exercise.

Meditate for Self-Acceptance

Self-acceptance involves training our minds, and we can do this through meditation, which is a valuable practice for self-esteem, helping us to become more present in our thoughts and calmer and more compassionate toward ourselves.

As I've said, my first meditation experiences weren't that successful. I thought the only way to meditate was to sit in silence in some sort of yoga position and have a still mind, where no thoughts entered or distracted you. I have a busy brain, so meditation didn't seem right for me.

But I found it helpful to bear in mind that we can't stop negative thoughts from popping into our minds, because our minds are naturally programmed to always be thinking, so it's natural for negative thoughts to still be present. However, as you become more attuned to the negative chatter, you can lovingly reject those thoughts and replace them with self-accepting ones. Again, the aim is to speak to yourself as you would a close friend. Chances are, you'd speak to them gently and sympathetically, no matter what they're going through.

Why not try the Developing Your Self-Acceptance Guided Meditation at the end of this step (*see pages 151–152*) and see if it helps you to become more in tune with your negative chatter and adopt self-acceptance?

Prioritize Self-Care

Integral to your journey toward self-acceptance is practicing self-love, self-care, and dedicating time to yourself. The terms 'self-care' and 'self-love' are often bandied around, but what do they actually mean? Self-care can mean engaging in different practices such as the small gestures we complete each day for ourselves, like brushing our teeth, combing our hair, eating a balanced diet, exercising, and so on, to the bigger acts of self-care – the more elaborate things we can do to care for ourselves, such as having a spa day, going on holiday, or engaging in other enjoyable activities. Many clients I work with realize during therapy that they struggle with the concept of allowing themselves the time and space for meaningful and conscious acts of self-care, but would benefit from it.

The key thing to remember is that self-love is about taking any action toward loving and caring for yourself in every way possible. If you can ingrain these practices into your life, they will help to reinforce a positive relationship with yourself. Even if at first you don't believe you can act from a place of self-love by applying self-care, such as through having a relaxing bath, doing a workout or meditating, you must demonstrate it to yourself in other ways, such as by taking a proper lunch break at work or getting a good night's sleep – these are things that demonstrate basic levels of showing love and care toward yourself.

When you prioritize time with yourself, this offers a precious opportunity to reconnect with yourself, reflect on your current life situation, and assess your needs and desires at any moment. Time alone can be spent in any way you enjoy most. It could be getting out in nature, having a reflective moment of mindfulness, journaling, preparing a wholesome meal, or enjoying a hot drink. The key is acknowledging the time you're carving out for yourself and making it purposeful.

'Me time,' the sacred space I carve out for myself, has been a lifeline in my journey. It offers a precious opportunity to reconnect with my inner self, reflect on my experiences, and recharge. Whether immersing myself in nature, indulging in a creative pursuit, or simply savoring a moment of tranquility, me time has become a sanctuary for self-discovery and growth, inspiring me to prioritize my well-being. Time alone may be especially rare if you have children, have other caring responsibilities, or work full-time. However, I have learned over the years that no matter how busy you might be, me time is essential to develop a better relationship with yourself.

Mindful Me Time

I would like you to create a list of intentional activities you can do independently. For example:

- doing something creative like artwork or crafts
- painting your nails
- cooking for pleasure

This week, I would like you to pick a day and time to spend this mindful time with yourself. This will help you connect with yourself more deeply and understand the importance of spending quality (intentional) time with yourself.

....

THERAPY AS SELF-LOVE

One of the biggest acts of self-love we can give ourselves is the space to explore our emotions in therapy. I may be biased because I'm a therapist, but I haven't always been one. As I shared earlier in this book, it was actually from my experience of attending therapy for the first time in my early 20s that I discovered the life-changing impact it can have on your life. It's a big statement to yourself to invest in therapy, and I don't only mean in terms of it being a financial investment. It's truly an acknowledgment that you're worth it, and that you're worth the time you're investing in yourself.

When I attended therapy for the first time, it allowed me to unearth the layers of my identity, emotions, and past and present experiences. It gave me a space to delve deep into my thoughts and feelings, and unravel some of the experiences in my life that had contributed to the person I am today. These included experiences that I saw as positive, but also those that had been difficult, such as being bullied or not feeling good enough, pretty enough, or like I fitted in anywhere because of my mixed heritage. Therapy can feel intense at times, because it involves revisiting painful memories or experiences. However, the process helped me to embrace my whole self – imperfections and all – and my journey so far.

Most people I work with come to therapy not feeling worthy of having my time – they minimize their problems and feel guilty for taking up the session. I always challenge my clients when this arises, of course, in a loving and supportive way. It makes no difference to your therapist if you come to therapy because you've burned a piece of toast or if you've suffered a terrible trauma of some kind. As therapists, we don't judge people on the seriousness of their issues. We understand that it's all about how the event impacts a person, and we care deeply about whatever your issue is; so please, if you ever feel like your problems aren't serious enough to go to a therapist, do think again. Going to therapy can help you uncover issues you may not even realize are profoundly impacting your life.

How to Find the Right Therapist

- Use reputable sources to find a therapist. This may be through your healthcare provider, health insurance, or employee assistance program at work.

- If you're seeking a private therapist not in these categories, use a therapy directory. This will ensure the therapists have been vetted and are fully qualified.

- The relationship you build with your therapist is key to therapy being effective, so make sure you feel comfortable with them. It may take a few sessions for you to know if they are the right fit. Please rest assured that it's OK to move to another therapist if you don't feel this is the right one for you. And any reputable therapist would encourage this.

••••

For me, the impact of self-acceptance has been immense. It's helped me to acknowledge my strengths and weaknesses without judgment, which I couldn't do before, have a better relationship with myself, and understand my needs. It's also allowed me to find inner peace and accept myself as I am, reducing the constant negative self-talk or criticism that had become an all-too-familiar way of being. The shift has allowed me to be kinder to myself and cultivate a more loving attitude toward myself. With this self-acceptance, I've also found it easier to adopt self-care practices. I ensure I meet my needs by doing activities like going to the gym and having sufficient rest and time alone.

Now that you've reached the end of this step, I hope you also feel better equipped to accept yourself for who you are. Please know that self-acceptance is a journey, not a destination. It's an ongoing process of loving and accepting who you are each day rather than a single event. It takes continued self-awareness, investing in yourself, and embracing the ever-changing human that you are.

I recommend a regular refresher of this step at intervals throughout the year, completing the exercises and making it a ritual to commit to yourself continuously. Our life experiences can influence our relationship with ourselves at any given time. The stronger our self-love, the stronger our resilience to the things that challenge us. If you want to join a community of like-minded people, then you may be interested in signing up for my Believe You're Made for More community at www.natashapagemsc.com.

Let's now get excited for the next part of our journey together as we embrace progression.

THERAPEUTIC EXERCISES

Embracing Imperfections

The objective of this exercise is to acknowledge and accept all parts of yourself.

I want you to write about those qualities, behaviors, or aspects of yourself that you find difficult to accept. For each one, reflect on its origins, how it has served you in some way, and how you can accept it as part of your whole self. For example:

> Sometimes I lose my patience with my family and I get frustrated with them, but I'm only human and it's OK not to be perfect. I may respond in this way because I'm trying to do my best as a mum and when I don't feel my family listen, I get annoyed. It's served me because I guess it's my way of trying to keep control over a situation.

> I don't feel confident in some aspects of my work, but I'm learning to understand them as best as I can. My lack of confidence stems from my school years – I wasn't very academic, so this makes me feel unsure about myself in work. It has served me to be cautious, because if people know I'm not confident, I feel like they won't blame me if I get things wrong.

End by writing self-acceptance affirmations, such as 'I'm human, and it's OK to be imperfect.'

Shadow Work

There are lots of books that cover this in much more depth, but the following exercise will give you an experience of the types of themes that shadow work can explore.

1. **Set an intention to engage in shadow work:** For example, is it to gain more clarity about your emotions, heal a part of yourself, or develop a better relationship with yourself? Write down your intention.

2. **Journal:** Use these journal prompts to dive into shadow work:

    - What qualities in others do you dislike or judge?
    - What situations or people evoke strong emotions in you?
    - When have you felt ashamed or guilty, and why?
    - What do you most fear people knowing about you?
    - What recurring negative patterns do you see in your life?
    - How does your inner child still show up in your life in the present?
    - What would your past self say to you to help you feel loved and supported?

3. **Tune in to your triggers:** We all have times when we may experience an emotional trigger to something; a strong reaction is often an insight into an unresolved aspect of the shadow self. An example may be the tone of voice someone uses when speaking to you; or if someone looks at you in a certain way, then you may make judgments about how they feel toward you. These experiences can provide insights into the aspects of ourselves that need emotional healing. For example, someone who has experienced bullying may be hyper-aware of how people respond to them, because they may have fears that they aren't liked.

4. **Communicate with the shadow self:** Internal dialogue with the shadow can involve writing a letter to a specific trait or visualizing a conversation with the shadow.

If this exercise involves deep traumas or intense emotions for you, I strongly encourage you to consider professional support. Therapists trained in shadow work or Jungian psychology can provide the care and guidance you need on this journey, ensuring you aren't alone in your exploration.

Shadow work is an ongoing process, not a one-time activity, as we continually grow, evolve, and develop our self-awareness and esteem. Other practices such as mindfulness meditation, art therapy, visualization, and body work are all helpful tools for engaging with the shadow.

Developing Your Self-Acceptance Guided Meditation

1. Make yourself comfortable. Close your eyes if this feels comfortable for you and focus on your breath. As you focus on your breath, breathe deeply and slowly. Stay like this for a few moments until you enter a deep state of relaxation.

2. As you breathe in, silently say, 'I am enough.' As you breathe out, think, 'I accept myself just as I am.' Repeat this affirmation with each breath, letting it sink deeper into your consciousness.

3. Imagine yourself standing in front of a mirror. In this mirror, you see your true self – your strengths, imperfections, light, and shadows. Everything is reflected to you with love and compassion.

4. As you look at yourself in the mirror, say to yourself, 'I love you and accept you.' Notice any feelings that arise. If any judgments occur, acknowledge them and let them go. Then, start repeating the affirmation: 'I love myself and accept myself just as I am.'

5. Take a moment to embrace all aspects of yourself, both the parts you love and the parts you struggle with. Imagine wrapping these parts of you in a bright white light, lovingly accepting them, and knowing that this light represents unconditional love and acceptance for yourself just as you are. Let it fill your entire body with a sense of love. Feel the warmth and love of this light as it embraces every part of you. Know that you are worthy of love and acceptance, just as you are.

6. Silently or out loud, repeat this affirmation: 'I accept myself, and I love myself.'

7. Allow this to resonate within you. Take a moment to feel grateful for yourself for honoring and accepting who you are.

8. Begin to bring your awareness back to your breath. Take a few deep, grounding breaths, feeling the air entering and leaving your body, and returning to the present moment with a sense of peace and self-acceptance. Feel the support beneath you, the air around you. Wiggle your fingers and toes, bringing movement back into your body. When you're ready, slowly open your eyes if they were closed, but keep the love and comfort you've experienced close to your heart.

9. Carry this feeling of acceptance with you as you go about your day, knowing that you are enough just as you are.

....

Affirm:
I embrace who I am and love myself just as I am.

EMBRACE PROGRESSION

Step 6

The sixth step is about trying new things that are good for you, embracing change, and evolving into the person you truly want to be.

This is my favorite step on our journey together. Embracing progression is about applying all the teachings we've covered so far – breaking free from the narratives you've told yourself, gaining a more profound sense of who you are, uncovering your authentic self, and accepting yourself for who you are – and stepping into the transformative process. In this phase, I can't promise that you'll remain in your comfort zone, because it's about quite the opposite; this is all about leaving it, trying new things, embracing change, and evolving into your desired self. This is essential to any form of personal growth and development, and to the next step of awakening to the higher self.

By the end of this step, I hope you will feel ready to progress toward achieving larger objectives and making your dreams a reality. Are you ready for change? I hope so.

BECOMING THE NEW YOU

The first step on your journey to discovering the new you is acknowledging where you are in the present. There may be aspects of life and yourself that you're pleased with, and also elements you want to change – this exercise will help you to uncover these.

Life Detox

Make a list of the areas in your life where you don't feel happy and the reasons why. For example:

- I'm unhappy with my weight at the moment. Why? Because I don't feel like I'm healthy.
- I'm not happy with my job. Why? Because I don't feel it fulfills me and I'm not earning the income I want to.
- I feel low, and I don't like myself much. Why? I've felt like this for a long time – I don't feel like I'm good enough.

Now, acknowledge the areas you feel happy or content with. Doing this can counterbalance the negative energy from the issues you are unhappy with. List the aspects of life you're grateful for. For example:

- I feel thankful for my good physical health.
- I appreciate my family and friends.
- I'm thankful I have a job.

I have used this exercise myself in periods of unhappiness or unease in my own life. As we explored in Step 3, gratitude is a powerful emotion that can help us cultivate a sense of appreciation for the positives in our lives, while still being realistic about the areas we want to change.

It's helpful to get crystal clear on the areas of your life that you aren't happy with, so that you have a starting point for what you want to change. Taking time to self-reflect is crucial to making positive changes in your life. I've often faced issues that I haven't been content with and, each time, the key to making a change was to sit and critically examine where things weren't aligning in my life. When leaving a job, self-reflection is required to help you realize it's time to move on. You begin to reflect on what makes you unhappy or feel stuck in your current job. When I tried to lose weight, I had to be honest with myself and agree that the food I was eating wasn't good for my body and I wasn't doing enough exercise.

Building your self-esteem and realizing how many things have been impacted by your low self-esteem may feel overwhelming initially, and people often need help figuring out where to start. It's essential to remember that transition takes time. This isn't an overnight thing; sometimes, acknowledging that you want to make a change is the most significant shift.

The last thing I want you to consider is that change always requires some risks. One of my favorite motivational sayings that I have up on my wall is: 'Take the risk or lose the chance.' This saying helped me move from thinking about leaving my secure corporate job and starting my own business, to doing it. Now, I'm not advising that you quit your job tomorrow – you might be extremely happy there! However, I encourage you to reflect on whether you're happy and content with where you are in your life right now. Think about other areas of your life where this is applicable. Do you need to take the risk and do something differently? Again, I'm not telling you what action to take – that isn't what I do as a therapist; however, I want to encourage you to be honest with yourself about which parts of your life still conform to what you think you should be living, rather than the life you truly want to live. For example, if there are issues in a relationship, you must ask yourself: Can these issues likely be worked upon and overcome? Could attending therapy, for example, help you make some changes or is it time to walk away kindly?

This reflection exercise can help you evaluate your life and clarify what you want to change. I would advise focusing on one or two changes at any given time, as trying to tackle everything all at once may lead to overwhelm. Often, small changes in one area of your life can lead to more significant changes overall.

I encourage you to approach this step with excitement and an abundance mindset. An abundance mindset is a way of thinking that focuses on the belief that everyone has enough resources and opportunities. This is contrary to the scarcity mindset we met in Step 2, which is rooted in the belief that resources are limited, leading to fear, competition, and anxiety. I want to acknowledge that sometimes people live in complex environments and inequality. However, an abundance mindset is still a powerful tool to adopt when working on making positive changes in your life.

To help you adopt an abundance mindset, identify the areas of your life you feel happy with. Focus on the innate potential you have within you as a human being, connect with nature and the beauty of the world, and know that the very act of reading this book marks the start of you living a more abundant life.

OVERCOME RESISTANCE TO CHANGE

Next, we need to explore something I see so many of my clients experiencing: resistance to change. It's likely that you'll be feeling this, too. One thing you should know is that it's natural to have some form of resistance. Often, when we want to change something in our lives, this can bring up conflicting emotions. We may feel a level of fear of the unknown and, consequently, worry about how the changes in us will impact those we love and care about. Change can lead to uncertainty, and this can feel scary. Sometimes, change can feel like hard work – think about people struggling with weight loss, for example. On the one hand, they want to change their bodies because they're not at their desired weight. However, they know that changing their body shape will require work, such as increasing their activities, exercising, and adjusting their food intake. For some, this can feel too daunting, so they give up early or don't even start. Ask yourself what resistance you've faced in the past or are feeling now when thinking about changing an area of your life.

Resistance to change is all linked to the mindset you create around the change. Our brains are wired to prefer routine and predictability, because this creates a sense of safety. As a result, we might experience feelings of anxiety, because our brains are hardwired to keep us safe from perceived harm. But remember, this is just an automatic response and, often, the change you want to create will far outweigh your present fears.

When it comes to overcoming any resistance, it can be helpful to understand your motivation for change...

Uncover Your Motivation for Change

There are two primary types of motivation:

1. **Extrinsic motivations** are the external incentives that compel you to act. These can include rewards such as money, praise, or recognition from others. They can also include avoiding negative consequences, such as punishment or disapproval. For example, you might work hard to earn a promotion or receive accolades from your peers.

2. **Intrinsic motivations** are the internal drivers that inspire you to take action because you find the activity itself rewarding. These

include personal growth, a sense of accomplishment, and the joy of learning or mastering a new skill. For example, you might feel a deep sense of satisfaction from completing a challenging project or helping others purely out of compassion.

Balancing these motivations can be the catalyst to overcoming resistance to change and making a start. Recognizing and valuing your intrinsic motivations – such as uncovering your why, how the change will benefit your life, and what personal values it aligns to – can help you find fulfillment and purpose in your actions. At the same time, understanding and leveraging extrinsic motivations can kick-start change and provide tangible rewards and acknowledgments that reinforce your efforts. Together, these create a comprehensive motivational framework that supports personal satisfaction and external achievements. This exercise will help you to uncover your motivation for change.

Indentifying Your Motivations for Change

1. Identify a change you want to make in your life. For example:

    I want to grow my business.

2. Identify any resistance you have to this. For example:

    I know being more active on social media will help grow my audience and potentially my sales, but I don't like being visible online.

3. Explore your extrinsic motivations (external factors):

    - Why should I make a change? For example:

    If I gain more followers, these are potential clients, which equal more money in my business.

- Why am I making a change? For example:

    My business friends have all told me I should do this.

- What could be a consequence if I don't do this? For example:

    People may choose my competitors over my services.

4. Explore your intrinsic motivations (internal drivers):

    - Why do I want this change? For example:

        It will help me to master a new skill and become better at an area in my business I don't have much experience of.

    - How would this impact my growth? For example:

        It will increase my confidence and help me to get out of my own way.

    - What would this allow me to experience more of in my life? For example:

        This will help me to enjoy the moment rather than seek external validation.

    - Would I still pursue this even if no one acknowledges or praises my achievement? For example:

        Yes, because this isn't about others; it's about me growing my business.

....

As with any change, there may be elements that make you feel uncomfortable, unfamiliar, and a little bit strange. Always remember that you aren't alone; if you're struggling, there are many qualified therapists/mental health professionals out there like me who can support you.

VISUALIZE YOUR IDEAL SELF

Our human form is meant to grow and evolve. Knowing this, you should acknowledge that you're a work in progress, as we all are. The person you are now will not be the same person you'll be in the next half an hour as you read this chapter. We're ever-evolving, absorbing new insights and growing into the highest version of ourselves each day. However, this evolution isn't just a process that happens on its own. It takes conscious actions and intentional steps to become the highest version of ourselves.

So, I ask you to take a moment and visualize the new you. You can create a road map for personal growth and transformation by imagining the person you want to become – this relates to how you feel about yourself and links to building better self-esteem. This higher version of yourself is doing precisely what you desire in life, earning the income you want, enjoying the holidays and activities you wish to do, and experiencing a spiritual connection that fills you with contentment, safety, and security. Does the new you have a different hair color? What job or business do they run? Does the new you have hobbies and interests? What food does the new you eat? What will they feel like inside: Are they content and happy in life? What does that look like for you? This exercise is designed to help you visualize and articulate your ideal self.

Visualizing Your Ideal Self

1. Find a quiet, comfortable space where you can reflect without distractions. Take a few deep breaths to center yourself.

2. Close your eyes if this feels comfortable for you and imagine yourself as the person you want to become. Picture yourself in vivid detail, focusing on different aspects of your life.

3. To help you visualize your ideal self, reflect on the following questions:

   What do you do?
   - How do you spend your day?
   - What activities and hobbies do you engage in?
   - What is your career or role in life?
   - How do you interact with others?

   What do you eat?
   - What are your favorite healthy foods?
   - How do you approach meals and nutrition?
   - Do you have any special routines around eating, such as cooking your own meals or eating mindfully?

   What is your mindset?
   - How does the new you respond to challenges and mistakes?
   - What things no longer align with who you're becoming?
   - What daily choices would the new you be making that you aren't making now?

   What do you look like?
   - How do you present yourself physically?
   - What is your style of clothing and grooming?
   - How do you carry yourself (posture, confidence)?
   - What kind of physical shape are you in, and how do you maintain it?

How does the new you align with your values?

- What brings the new you joy?
- How do you achieve more in your life?
- When do you feel most like yourself? How can you cultivate that feeling more often?
- If you were feeling fear or self-doubt, how would you move past this?

4. Open your eyes if they were closed and record your reflections. Describe in detail the new you. For example:

- **Daily activities:** In my ideal day, I wake up early and start with a morning workout. I spend my day working on meaningful projects and make time for hobbies like painting and reading.
- **Diet:** My diet consists of fresh, whole foods. I enjoy cooking my own meals and make a point to include a variety of vegetables, lean proteins, and whole grains.
- **Mindset:** I feel confident and capable of achieving my goals.
- **Appearance:** I take care of my physical health by exercising regularly and maintaining a balanced diet. I dress in a way that expresses my personality, favoring comfortable yet stylish clothing.
- **Alignment:** I feel like I'm living my purpose. I'm content in the person I am and evolving to be.

SHED THE OLD YOU

One of the most challenging decisions I had to make in my own life was when I separated from my first husband. Despite several encounters where I could have easily left and a catalogue of evidence supporting my decision to leave, it was still a tough decision. I vividly recall contemplating what other people would think. I didn't want to be seen as another single mum, and I was worried about my daughter and the impact it would have on her if her dad and I separated. I worried about my finances and desperately battled with what life might be like if I did leave. Would I lose my home or have no money? I had to face the harsh realities of the outcomes and was prepared to accept them. I even knew this could have meant moving back to my parents' house at the age of 29, and that wasn't something I'd ever imagined having to do. But even with all of these anxieties, I knew deep down that if I continued in the relationship, I wouldn't be honoring myself. I would be living a life to keep others happy, and that is a dangerous game, because we can't ever be responsible for someone else's happiness, only our own.

Yes, there was heartache. Yes, it was so difficult and the hardest thing I've ever done, but God/the Universe, or whatever feels most fitting to your beliefs, stepped in soon enough. I had confirmation that the relationship should end when my ex slept with someone else just a week after we'd separated, and this, for me, helped me to know I'd made the right decision. There was no turning back at that point. My self-respect wouldn't allow it, and this sealed my decision. Financially, I would be OK. After finishing university, I started a full-time job as a mature student and was lucky to claim working tax credits as a single mum. This enabled me to remain in my family home and pay the mortgage independently. My proudest moment was taking on the mortgage solely in my name, and I give thanks to God, because it felt like I'd been given the support and resources

I needed. This, to me, was further confirmation that I had done the right thing.

To become the new you, you must shed old habits, limiting beliefs, and things you used to conform to. It doesn't have to be the end of a relationship. It could be the shedding of old habits and patterns that aren't serving you. It could be a toxic friendship, a job you hate, an addiction, or numerous other issues that may arise in your life. It's time to shed the old self and step into a new version of yourself – and you will decide what that looks like. You're the one to decide who you want to be. Reinvention is a process that requires deliberate actions repeated over time, until you become the version of what you constantly desire to be. This is the version of yourself that you were born to be and meant to be all along.

Creating a Vision Board

A vision or action board can be a wonderful way to tap into the new experiences you want to bring into your life. This exercise complements the one we did earlier when we visualized our ideal self, but, this time, you're creating a visual representation of the things you want to attract into your life. Vision boards can help to evoke excitement, motivation, and commitment to seeing your dreams come to fruition.

Remember, it's OK to dream. Let your mind go wild. Don't hold yourself back from putting down exactly what your heart desires. Even if these things feel out of reach right now, the whole point of this exercise is to allow yourself to dream, so why not dream BIG?

There are no right or wrong suggestions for your vision board – it's a really fun opportunity to get clear on your goals and vision for your future self. Exciting! Here are some ideas that you might want to include to inspire you and get you started:

- writing a bestselling book
- running a thriving business
- earning six- or seven-figure income
- starting an impactful charity or movement that inspires many
- achieving a fitness goal or transformation
- appearing on a famous talk show
- helping millions across the globe
- giving a large amount of money away to a meaningful charity
- doing a sky dive
- traveling the world

•••••••••••••••••••

Every day, I take great pleasure in seeing my targeted vision in front of me. This fuels excitement about what I am working toward and what's possible. I can tell you that on my vision board at the beginning of 2024, I stuck a photo that represented a book being published, and I wrote '2024' on top of my board. Weeks after putting this on my board, I took action. I'd submitted my revised book proposal just before Christmas. I proposed to the editing team that they should let me know the next steps if they liked the idea. I expected them to return and either say no, the idea didn't work for them, or that they would like me to proceed to write two chapters. But guess what? They surprised me with an enthusiastic and resounding YES. Receiving that email was an unforgettable experience. I was jumping up and down with excitement in the kitchen. My children sensed something was up, and I was excited to share the good news with them!

SET ACTIONABLE GOALS

A crucial element of change is knowing you can't just wake up one morning and say, 'I'm not going to have low self-esteem anymore!' This is because you'll still have days when you feel unkind toward yourself. Therefore, it's helpful to acknowledge that an issue such as self-esteem won't be solved immediately and instead set more achievable, measurable goals, such as saying, for example, 'I'll speak kindly to myself, starting by saying one positive affirmation once a day.' These small, conscious changes lead to a more significant transformation.

To set actionable goals, first identify two to three specific changes you can start making today to move toward the ideal self you visualized in the exercises on pages 162–164 and 166–167. For example: 'I'll start by incorporating a 30-minute walk into my daily routine.'

Then, create a simple plan to achieve your goals. Break down each goal into smaller, manageable steps. For example: 'This week I'll start with a 30-minute walk twice a week. Then, I'll add another day each week when I'm ready to increase this. Then, I'll work up to a 30-minute walk each day.'

Acknowledging the new habits that must be established to make real and lasting changes in your life is crucial. For example, in my journey to become an author, I had to form strong habits of showing up and writing daily. This process was a conscious decision to become an author – showing up every day to add more insight onto the empty pages of my Word document. Only two years ago, I couldn't envisage myself as an author who would write every day.

But I started first with small steps, committing to writing at least a few times a month, and, as I developed my book proposal, I began to write more regularly. It then turned into a habit, one result of which is the crafting of this very book over the past nine months. This sometimes meant just writing a paragraph, sometimes editing, or, on more productive days, writing hundreds or even thousands of words.

I share this example to demonstrate that change is not a one-off event. It's a conscious lifestyle shift that requires daily commitment, until it becomes so ingrained in your life that it is non-negotiable – it's just a part of who you are. Research has found that neuroplasticity means the brain can change and adapt due to experience.[18] The result of this is that we can create change, reorganize, or grow our neural networks. This is positive news, because it shows we can establish new ways of living and being. We don't have to believe things will be like this forever, just because they are the way they are right now. You have the power to change and evolve your mind and life.

We must decide whether to stay in our comfort zone or take a leap and do something different. Many people wait until they feel ready for something, but that day may never come. As Susan Jeffers says in her classic guide *Feel the Fear and Do It Anyway*, by feeling the fear and doing things despite it, we start to cultivate confidence and gain more clarity when we begin to take action. In my experience, there will likely be obstacles along the way and moments when you feel uncertain or stuck. Turning daydreams into actions transforms them into goals, and there will be moments of fear and doubt. But these are also the moments when the most significant breakthroughs can

---

18   Psychology Today Staff, 'Neuroplasticity' (n.d.): www.psychologytoday.com/gb/basics/neuroplasticity [Accessed September 26, 2025].

be achieved – when you declare to the Universe how much you want something and you chase it no matter what. This is also where work on your mindset comes in, as you need to start viewing things differently. When you face a hurdle such as rejection, try not to see it as this but as a cue to redirect you and allow you to do things differently. When things aren't working to your desired timeline, it's about trusting in the process and knowing that things will either work out in their divine timing or that there may be another path you're destined to take.

Make sure you review and adjust your goals periodically. Reflect on your progress and make adjustments as needed. This ongoing process will help you stay on track as you move toward your ideal self.

Zainab's Story

Zainab, a 28-year-old teacher, sought therapy due to persistent feelings of low self-esteem, dissatisfaction with her career, and challenges in her personal relationships. She described a pattern of self-doubt, negative self-talk, and a lack of confidence that was impacting her overall well-being and quality of life.

By focusing on self-esteem, self-worth, and personal growth, she entered a transformative phase marked by a deep commitment to change and a willingness to challenge her limiting beliefs. She wanted to break free from the cycle of negativity and embrace a more empowered and fulfilling life.

She started incorporating daily positive affirmations into her routine, focusing on self-love, acceptance, and empowerment. These affirmations also helped her challenge negative thoughts and cultivate a more positive mindset.

I encouraged Zainab to try journaling regularly as a tool for self-reflection and emotional processing. This involved her writing down her thoughts and feelings, which allowed her to gain clarity, express herself authentically, and identify areas for personal growth. She started prioritizing her self-care by engaging in activities that nourished her mind, body, and soul. These included regular exercise, healthy eating, practicing mindfulness, and setting aside time for relaxation and hobbies she enjoyed. She learned to set healthy boundaries in her relationships and prioritize her own needs and well-being. She communicated assertively and respectfully, which led to more rewarding and balanced connections with others. Feeling unfulfilled in her teaching job, she explored new career opportunities that aligned with her passions and strengths. She enrolled in professional development courses, networked with industry professionals, and took proactive steps toward transitioning into a career that brought her greater fulfillment and satisfaction.

The changes and new actions Zainab implemented had a profound impact on her life. She reported a significant increase in her self-confidence, self-worth, and overall happiness. Her relationships improved, as she set healthier boundaries and communicated her needs more effectively. Her career transition brought a renewed sense of purpose and achievement, allowing her to pursue her professional goals with confidence and enthusiasm.

Her journey from struggling with low self-esteem to embracing personal transformation exemplifies the power of resilience, self-discovery, and intentional change. Through her dedication, Zainab broke free from limiting beliefs, cultivated a positive self-image, and created a life filled with meaning, purpose, and fulfillment.

••••

Now we've come to the end of this step, it's time for the fun part – get ready to start making changes and living the life you truly desire! There are some suggestions on how to start taking action in the following therapeutic exercises. This should be approached with fun and enjoyment. It isn't a one-size-fits-all approach. Remember, you are your unique self, and some of these suggestions may not align with what you want. And that's fine. The whole point is to explore what lights you up. It's simply about having the chance to reflect on what you are most drawn to and then going with it.

This part of your journey is a stepping stone to the final chapter – awakening the higher self. When we start to make positive changes in our life, we ignite the parts of us that open the pathways to the higher self. Think about how you feel when you're in your happiest state and are engaged in activities that you enjoy, whether that's art, reading, writing, cooking, walking in nature, traveling, volunteering, meditating, journaling, or dance – I imagine you feel joy, elation, and contentment. These are all higher-self states. I encourage you to dig deep and find the thing(s) that light up your soul before progressing to the next step.

THERAPEUTIC EXERCISES

How Ready Are You for Change?

Take this questionnaire to gauge how ready you are to make changes in your life. (*You can also access this questionnaire at www.natashapagemsc.com.*)

Firstly, identify an area of your life where you feel unhappy or unfulfilled, or that you would like to improve.

Now, answer these questions in your journal or jot them down on a piece of paper:

1. **How unhappy are you with your current circumstances?**

    Very unhappy (**4**)

    Somewhat unhappy (**3**)

    Neutral (**2**)

    Somewhat OK (**1**)

    Satisfied (**0**)

2. **How strong is your desire to make this change?**

    Very strong (**4**)

    Somewhat strong (**3**)

    Neutral (**2**)

    Not very strong (**1**)

    Weak (**0**)

3. **What are the consequences if you don't make this change?**

    I will feel very unhappy (**4**)

    I will feel somewhat unhappy (**3**)

    I feel nothing much at all (**2**)

    I'll feel somewhat OK (**1**)

    I'll feel satisfied (**0**)

4. **How confident are you about making the change happen?**

    Extremely confident (**4**)

    Very confident (**3**)

    Neutral (**2**)

A little unsure (**1**)

Not confident in the slightest (**0**)

5. **How easy do you find adapting to change?**

   Very easy (**4**)

   I can do it, but I sometimes find it challenging (**3**)

   I often find it difficult (**2**)

   I resist change unless I have to (**1**)

   I avoid change (**0**)

6. **Do you need support to aid this change and, if so, do you feel you have adequate support?**

   I have a strong support system (**4**)

   I have some support (**3**)

   I have minimal support (**2**)

   I feel alone in this (**1**)

   I have no support at all (**0**)

7. **Do you feel prepared to take action toward the change?**

   I have already started to take action (**4**)

   I have a plan in place I need to start (**3**)

   I want to take action, but I'm not sure how to start (**2**)

   I'm not ready to make a change yet, but will be one day (**1**)

   I'm not going to take action at all (**0**)

8. **How do you view challenges that may come your way?**

   I'm ready for a challenge: I can do this (**4**)

I expect challenges and feel OK about this (**3**)

I feel anxious about facing challenges (**2**)

I think challenges may hinder my progress (**1**)

I can't handle the challenges that may come along the way (**0**)

9. **Are you committed to making change in your life?**

   Yep, I'm 100 percent committed – I won't let anyone stop me (**4**)

   I'm very committed (**3**)

   I want to be committed, but I don't feel confident I'll remain so (**2**)

   Not very committed (**1**)

   I'm not committed in the slightest (**0**)

10. **How excited are you about the benefits this change could bring?**

    Extremely excited! (**4**)

    Very excited (**3**)

    Somewhat excited (**2**)

    A little excited but also unsure (**1**)

    Not excited at all (**0**)

Scoring Guide

32–40 points: You're fully ready for change!

24–31 points: You're almost there, but just need a little clarity or support.

15–23 points: You have some hesitation – what's holding you back?

Below 15 points: You might not be ready yet. What fears or doubts do you need to address first?

Starting to Take Action

Here are some suggestions on how to start taking action to make positive changes in your life. Pick one or two you feel drawn to and go ahead and do them. This is the start of creating your new reality, so embrace the process and enjoy it.

- **Create a bucket list:** Write down everything you've always wanted to do – places you want to visit, skills you want to learn, and so on. This can serve as a road map for your new experiences.

- **Set goals:** Break down your bucket list items into actionable goals. For example, if you want to travel to four new countries in the next two years, set a goal to visit one country every six months.

- **Explore your interests:** Try out new hobbies or revisit old ones that you used to enjoy. This could be something like painting, dancing, hiking, or cooking.

- **Step out of your comfort zone:** Challenge yourself by doing things that scare you a little (but are safe and legal, of course). This could be public speaking, trying exotic foods, or taking a solo trip.

- **Travel:** Whether it's a weekend getaway to a nearby town or a month-long adventure to a foreign country, travel exposes you to new cultures, people, and experiences, so make a plan to travel in ways that suit you and your budget.

- **Attend events and workshops:** Look for local events, workshops, and seminars that relate to your interests. This is a great way to meet like-minded people and expand your knowledge.

- **Volunteer:** Giving back to your community or volunteering for causes you believe in can be incredibly rewarding and eye-opening, so research the opportunities to do this either locally or nationally.

- **Read widely:** Explore books, articles, and blogs on topics you're curious about. Reading expands your knowledge and can inspire new ideas and perspectives.

- **Say 'yes' more often:** Be open to opportunities that come your way. Sometimes, saying 'yes' to things you normally wouldn't agree to can lead to amazing experiences. Always be mindful of your boundaries, though, and don't say 'yes' to things when it really is a 'no'. Check in with yourself and ensure the reasons you want to say 'yes' are aligned with your authentic self or your self-development.

- **Document your journey:** Keep a journal or blog or vlog about your experiences. Reflecting on your journey can help you appreciate how far you've come and inspire you to keep trying new things.

- **Connect with people:** Build relationships with diverse groups of people. You can learn a lot from others' experiences and perspectives.

- **Practice mindfulness:** Stay present and mindful in your day-to-day life. Paying attention to the small moments can bring a sense of fulfillment and appreciation for life's experiences.

Remember, staying curious, open-minded, and proactive in seeking new experiences is key. These are meant to be fun and enrich your life experience and build your confidence and esteem. Try new things that are good for you, embrace change, and evolve into the person you truly want to be.

Embracing Progression Guided Meditation

1. Make yourself comfortable. Close your eyes if this feels comfortable for you and focus on your breath. As you focus on your breath, breathe deeply and slowly. Stay like this for a few moments until you enter a deep state of relaxation.

2. As you breathe in, silently say, 'I am making progress.' As you breathe out, think, 'I embrace this evolution.' Repeat this affirmation with each breath, letting it sink deeper into your consciousness.

3. Now, bring your attention to the prospect of change. Change is a part of life, an essential element. As you focus on your breath, welcome the idea of change into your heart. Change is a sign of growth, evolution, progress, and new opportunities.

4. Visualize yourself at the start of a long, winding path. This path represents your journey through change. The path has many twists and turns, and you can't quite determine where it will take you. As you walk along the route, you come to an opening, a vast green field; you stop for a moment and take in the unfolding beauty and wonder of the path ahead.

5. Allow yourself to feel any emotions that arise – whether it's excitement, fear, or uncertainty. Acknowledge these feelings with compassion and understanding. They are a natural part of embracing change.

6. As you continue walking along the path, imagine that, with each step, you're shedding old layers of yourself –

old beliefs or patterns that no longer serve you. These layers fall away easily, like petals falling from a flower.

7. With each breath, envision yourself evolving into a better version of yourself. See yourself growing more aligned with your purpose. Feel the energy of transformation flowing through you, empowering you to embrace your full potential.

8. Imagine yourself standing in a beautiful spot within the field. This is the place where your highest self resides, and where you know all things are possible. Take a moment to connect with this version of yourself. Feel the inner power and quiet confidence, and embrace progression.

9. Repeat silently or aloud, whichever feels right for you, the following affirmations:

    - 'I embrace progression as a natural part of my journey.'

    - 'I am evolving into the best version of myself.'

    - 'I trust the process of progressing at my own pace.'

    - 'I release what no longer serves me and embrace my true purpose.'

10. Take a few deep breaths and embrace these affirmations in your heart. When you feel ready, slowly bring your awareness back to the present moment and open your eyes if they were closed.

11. Carry this sense of optimism with you as you move through your day. Remember, you have the power within, and, as you progress through this phase of your life, know that you have the quiet confidence within that all will work out.

....

Affirm:
I embrace change and evolve into the person I want to be.

AWAKEN THE HIGHER SELF

Step 7

The seventh step is tapping into your non-material dimension, soul and spirit – the part of you unencumbered by ego – and connecting with your higher self so you can reach your full potential.

You've been on a journey through each step before this one to raise your levels of self-esteem. And, after all the strides you've taken in pursuit of your personal growth, you've finally reached the pinnacle – the seventh step: awakening the higher self. To build true self-esteem, none of the previous steps can be ignored and you have drawn closer to your higher self with each step you've taken.

Now you've reached this point, we'll delve into discovering your spiritual self and its relevance to self-esteem, before exploring how you can live spiritually and step into your higher power. I'm not here to preach my views on religion and so, whatever your religious or spiritual beliefs may be, or even if you have none, it's simply my hope that this step will help you to reflect on what gives your life significance, guiding you as you explore your purpose and helping you to illuminate the path to a more meaningful life. Before this awakening, you may have been led by your ego's thoughts, which, as we've explored, leads to low self-esteem. As you start to live a life with more purpose and meaning, you will be liberated from the fear and self-doubt of the ego and, instead, are led by your higher self. You realize that you have the freedom and responsibility to shape your own destiny, sparking positive change, growth, and development.

Living from your higher self is essential for your self-esteem, as it will instill in you a sense of inherent worth that isn't governed by the ego and guide you further toward the positive self-perception you've been working so hard to build in the previous steps.

This final step will encourage you to reach for your wildest dreams and manifest your heart's desires, filling you with hope and optimism for the future.

Defining a Higher Power

A higher power is a concept with many meanings and no exact definition. Some people believe a higher power is a deity or supernatural being, such as a god, while others think it's Mother Nature or the Universe. Other people view a higher power as an abstract idea, such as love, music, or consciousness.

Throughout this step, I will refer to God for my own experiences, but you may feel more aligned with using whatever term feels comfortable for you: the Source, the divine, your higher power, and so on.

I would now like you to consider your interpretation of a higher power. What do you think of when we say higher power? Use whatever creative medium appeals to you to create a visual or written statement, symbol, or drawing to describe your belief in a higher power.

WHAT IS THE HIGHER SELF?

When I refer to the higher self, I'm talking about the purest and most authentic version of you – the most empowered and confident version that isn't governed by the ego, fear, and anxiety, or the expectations of others; it doesn't conform to the social norms or care what others think. In spiritual terms, the higher self is often understood as our innate worth – it's the part of us that only we can tune in to.

Some of you reading this may not have specific beliefs, which is fine. You may even find this topic a little 'woo-woo' and don't consider spirituality to be your thing. However, in my experience, most people question the purpose and meaning of their lives at some point in their journey. For some, this thought may result in no change; they may even dismiss it and not delve any deeper. For others, though, this curiosity will spark an innate belief that there's more to life than the physical realm of this Universe and they may resonate with the inner knowing that they are truly made for more.

When we recognize our inherent value, we connect to the higher self, the innate version deep within our soul. This higher self helps us to understand that true confidence and self-esteem come from recognizing we're meant for more. This is an awakening to the potential you hold within yourself, and that you're capable of much more than you know. The higher version of yourself is open to the possibilities that life has to offer, and is living your life fully aligned with your purpose. Connecting with your higher self unlocks your potential to be the most expansive version of yourself. The higher self knows their worth, capabilities, and influence on the world around them.

THE HIGHER SELF AND THE CONNECTION TO SELF-ESTEEM

Spirituality can have several positive effects on our self-esteem:

- It can provide a sense of belonging and purpose beyond material success or external validation. This can help us feel more fulfilled and satisfied with our lives and improve our self-esteem.

- Many spiritual practices use the cultivation of positive emotions such as love, compassion, and gratitude, which, as we've now explored, help us feel better about ourselves and, in turn, boost our self-esteem.

- A key element of building self-esteem is to love and accept ourselves and others. Spirituality often encourages us to adopt forgiveness and acceptance. This can help us become less critical of ourselves and change our negative thinking patterns.

- Adopting practices such as prayer and meditation help induce relaxing states and a sense of inner peace and calm, reducing stress and anxiety. Consequently, they help boost your self-esteem, too.

- Spirituality can help us cultivate a more profound sense of self-worth and inner peace, positively impacting our self-esteem.

It's said that the three components of spirituality are 'meaning and purpose in life,' 'mission in life,' and 'altruism,' implying that our sense of purpose in life directly correlates with our mental health and well-being – and I truly believe that when you connect to your higher self, you can access a deeper understanding of your true potential and value.

If we center our lives on the spirit that dwells within, we can live with hearts full of self-acceptance and the belief that we're made for more. It can raise our self-esteem and make our earthly challenges less arduous.

Now, low self-esteem may have once stopped you from reaching for your dreams or fulfilling your true purpose in life. However, it doesn't have to remain this way. YOU possess the extraordinary ability to create the life of your dreams. The more you build your self-esteem, the more you'll begin to embody a sense of inner peace, quiet confidence, and an inner knowing that when you listen to the silent dwellings within your heart, they will lead you to a more authentic and fulfilling life. Connecting to your spiritual side and aligning your thoughts, beliefs, and actions with your goals and ambitions can shape the reality you desire and deserve. Remember, YOU have the divine power within you; you can change, evolve, and become the best version of yourself.

THE STAGES OF SPIRITUAL AWAKENING

Spiritual awakening is often described as a profound realization or enlightenment. It's a process where you 'wake up' to the true essence of life. During this journey, many questions emerge, and you begin to sense that life holds much more depth and meaning than you previously believed. Awakening involves an unfolding process unique to your journey. People often experience a similar unfolding of awakening in five stages:

Stage 1: Unconsciousness

Initially, the ego's guidance causes life to flow from unconsciousness. This means our social conditioning heavily influences our actions. We view the world through a subjective lens. We're frequently led by our automatic ways of thinking, which are usually rooted in the narrative we've built over time (we explored this in Steps 1 and 2). These thoughts influence our beliefs, roles, and actions in life. Also, they're often not in line with our higher selves.

Stage 2: Ego Death

Awakening involves the stage of ego death. This can occur at critical junctures, such as when we're faced with a significant life shift or traumatic experience. It may lead to the realization that everything previously taken as a fixed entity dissipates.

These previously held self-perceptions and old narratives start to shed, and concepts of who and what we once were change. The suffering experienced from these events becomes easier to let go of. You did a lot of work on rejecting those old narratives in Step 3.

Ego death results in a tireless search for purpose and meaning. Consequently, long-held limiting beliefs lose their grip and a new world of possibilities is unearthed. Ego death can be profoundly unsettling for those people who experience it, but it's essential for rebirth to begin.

Stage 3: The Search

The search prompts us to question our purpose in life and understand our existence. Many of us will embark on a journey of self-discovery and research. We'll access teachings from others, read books, and engage in different practices and experiences to help us understand, in essence, our non-physical selves. This is where heightened awareness and insights are gained. In Steps 4 and 5, you explored the importance of your authentic self, connecting more to the essence of who you truly are, and developing self-acceptance.

Stage 4: Emergence of the True Self

With our new understanding and perspective of the world, the ego transforms into a catalyst for the higher self. We begin to release the outdated versions of ourselves, shedding former personas and ways of being. This links to our work earlier in Step 6. We try new things and embrace a new perspective of ourselves and how we want to live our lives. As we do this, our higher selves are revealed. Our innate gifts and purpose come to light, guiding us into unwavering alignment. Living from a place of infinite potential, we fully embrace our role as co-creators of our reality. This unlocks new possibilities and allows us to discover our true capabilities, turning our dreams into reality through our aligned actions.

Stage 5: Life of Alignment

As we awaken to the pure essence of life, our consciousness expands and we start to experience the world in an entirely new way. Enlightenment is when we align with our purpose, begin to see beyond the physical, and recognize the shared spiritual foundation that connects us all – the focus of this final step. This is when we really start to connect with our higher self and realize our need to nurture this part of ourselves. We see ways to enhance our spiritual well-being through the development of our spiritual practices, such as meditation and prayer, so we can sit, be still, focus within, and connect with our higher self. We observe others through a lens of compassion and kindness, and despite our physical or personality differences, we have an intrinsic capacity to love and empathize with one another. This acknowledges the shared spiritual energy that binds us and the inherent equality of every human being. We want to connect more with nature and have a heightened awareness of our connection to the natural world. This experience in nature mirrors the spiritual truth that we're all part of a greater whole, each with our unique form but fundamentally the same in essence.

Where Are You in Your Awakening?

1. Take some time to sit down and reflect on where you feel you are in your awakening and why.

2. Describe a recent experience where you felt a deep sense of spirituality or connection to something greater than yourself.

3. How do your spiritual beliefs influence your emotional well-being and self-esteem?

CHECK IN ON YOUR SPIRITUAL WELLNESS

Have you ever felt lacking in spiritual connectedness and questioned how this relates to your own sense of self? In what ways do you think about yourself? Do you truly and deeply love and accept yourself? If not, why not?

You may already be doing this, but checking in on your spiritual wellness is always helpful, no matter what stage you're at. Spiritual wellness is our health in a spiritual context. So, for some, this may relate to religion, but it may also be things such as your connection to the natural world, connections with others, and living in alignment with the values you identified in Step 4 (*see pages 100–104*). Whatever spiritual wellness looks like for you, it involves a connection between you and something greater than yourself. It's a connection to God, Mother Nature, or the Universe; a sense of meaning, purpose, values, and beliefs. Having good levels of spiritual wellness can positively impact your self-esteem.

There are some exercises throughout this chapter to help strengthen your spirituality, but a good starting point is to ask yourself the following questions to determine if you suffer from low spiritual esteem:

- Do you experience feelings of emptiness, as though your life lacks meaning?

- Do you often experience anxiety and general feelings of unsettledness?

- Do you usually feel that you need to improve yourself, or do you feel the opposite, feeling unconcerned about life?

- Do you lack a general sense of inner peace and belonging?

- Do you find it hard to be compassionate toward yourself and others?

If any of these issues resonate with you, you may be experiencing poor spiritual wellness, which is contributing to your low self-esteem.

Regardless of whether you suffer from low spiritual esteem or not, this step will help you strengthen your connection to your higher power. It will instill in you the belief that anything is possible when you tap into your non-material dimension, soul and spirit, and connect with your divine.

WHAT IT LOOKS LIKE TO LIVE AS YOUR HIGHER SELF

When we are aligned and living from our higher self, we're living in our most authentic state. This means we can show up just as we are and are no longer driven by the need to please others or seek validation from external sources. We can be bold and step into the world facing our fears and embracing all that life has to offer. This doesn't mean that we don't ever get nervous or face challenges – trust me, I still do – but it does mean that we're able to rise to the challenge and hold a calm confidence within us that everything will turn out all right. We can act on our dreams and pursue life with zeal.

The higher self operates from a place of abundance, tapping into the things we feel gratitude for and believing that there is more than enough, and that we're deserving of all the good things coming our way. The higher self acts in alignment with our values and purpose. When making decisions, we're quicker to act from our intuition, trusting that voice within rather than seeking the approval of others. We develop a greater understanding of our needs and we embrace and love ourselves just as we are – even the parts of us we know aren't perfect – because we know that the human condition isn't perfect and it's all part of the journey toward our highest self.

In my own life, I've experienced ebbs and flows in my journey toward the higher self. Sometimes, I feel spiritually rich, while I feel less so at other times. What I do know is that whenever I live from the higher self, I feel happy and content. I believe in myself and experience more flow and ease in my life. I'm not struggling and striving for things. I accept the things I can positively influence and take action toward them. My relationships are in a better place and I have more energy for my loved ones. I feel more connected, more present, calmer, and happier.

BARRIERS TO ACCESSING THE HIGHER SELF

We've already explored how low self-esteem makes you doubt yourself and who you are, but it can also make it very challenging to be open about topics that can cause ambiguity, because you never know what other people's reactions will be. You worry that others will judge and think badly of you. You also fear that they won't accept you and will reject you – and this can become a major barrier to accessing the higher self.

I was raised as a Christian and have openly declared my belief in God to people who don't have the same perspective and beliefs. This has been difficult for me and uncomfortable at times. Not everybody will have the same viewpoint, be spiritual, or believe in God – and that's fine. However, it becomes essential for your spiritual development to be open about who you are. This goes hand in hand with increasing your self-esteem and living as your authentic self, which we explored in Step 4. Over the years, I've realized that when we aren't open about our beliefs and connection with a higher being, we're denying ourselves, and there's nothing worse than that. From my own experiences and observations of clients in therapy, it's evident that it's essential to have like-minded people with whom you feel you can be fully open about your spirituality alongside you on this journey. This not only feeds into your spiritual growth, but also into your self-esteem and enables you to take those first steps toward accessing the higher self.

The more you build a positive relationship with your higher self, the more you'll notice how others will respond to you accordingly. Those who love you will be excited to see your growth in self-esteem. Those who may not be aligned with you, and probably never will be, may drop off the radar or have negative reactions to your growth. Know that this shedding of old relationships that don't serve you anymore is OK. It's safe to let go of those people and things that no longer serve your evolving self.

Our spirit, intuition, and soul's inner compass lead the higher self, but accessing it can sometimes feel like an impossible challenge. In a world that can be very distracting, we're all so busy and live in such a fast-paced society that we can quickly become stuck in a self-perpetuating cycle of mundane activities that mean we seldom experience real joy and connection to the higher self. Accessing the higher self becomes even harder when you experience low self-esteem, because you may feel even more disconnected from this part of you. However, within all of us is a dwelling that houses our higher self.

Connecting with our higher power means intentionally connecting with this part of us. I feel most attuned to my higher self when I feel a sense of connecting to God. This is often when I'm in nature, near the sea, in prayer, or meditating. For many who relate to a sense of spirituality, rituals or practices similarly help them to express or connect with their higher selves. As part of your journey to overcoming barriers and raising your self-esteem, I encourage you to develop your own spiritual practices, too. Remember, this is *your* spiritual journey and your spiritual practices will be unique to you. They may be connected to your religious beliefs or they may not. Whatever the case is for you, I encourage you to use this exercise to find the things that feel most aligned with you.

Developing Your Own Spiritual Practices

Developing your spiritual practices can help you connect to your higher self. For example, practicing a religion may mean attending a place of worship regularly or praying. It can also involve other practices, such as those in the following list. Dedicating time to these is vital. This is the starting point for allowing yourself to devote time to your spiritual self.

You'll see from the list that there are a great many different ways that people can find a connection to their spiritual selves. You may already be engaging in some of these; if you are, that's great. Maybe you could try something new from the list, too?

- **Meditation:** regularly setting aside quiet time for reflection and mindfulness
- **Prayer:** engaging in personal or communal prayer
- **Reading sacred texts:** studying religious scriptures or spiritual writings
- **Nature walks:** spending time in nature to feel a sense of connection with the Universe
- **Gratitude journaling:** writing down things you're thankful for each day
- **Attending worship services:** participating in religious ceremonies or services
- **Yoga:** practicing yoga to align the body and mind
- **Acts of service:** volunteering or helping others in need
- **Listening to inspirational music:** enjoying music that uplifts and inspires
- **Mindful breathing:** practicing deep and mindful breathing exercises
- **Art and creativity:** expressing yourself through art, music or writing
- **Community fellowship:** engaging with a spiritual or religious community
- **Spiritual retreats:** attending retreats for deeper spiritual immersion
- **Positive affirmations:** repeating affirmations to cultivate a positive mindset
- **Contemplation:** reflecting on life's purpose and the mysteries of existence

- **Pilgrimages:** visiting sacred sites or places of spiritual significance
- **Fasting:** engaging in fasting as a spiritual discipline
- **Chanting or affirmations:** repeating sacred sounds or phrases
- **Mindful eating:** eating with awareness and gratitude
- **Visualization:** imagining a connection with your higher power

These practices can help deepen your spiritual awareness and foster a stronger connection with your higher power. Which ones do you feel most drawn to, and why?

Here are detailed descriptions of two suggested activities from the list, along with guidance on how to engage in these practices. If you wish, write down any thoughts, emotions, or insights that arise for you during these exercises. Reflect on how these experiences made you feel.

Listening to Inspirational Music

Allow 15 to 30 minutes for this exercise.

1. Choose a quiet, comfortable place where you won't be disturbed.
2. Sit or lie down in a relaxed position.
3. Before starting, take a moment to set an intention for your listening experience. This could be anything from seeking inner peace, to connecting with a higher power, or simply being present with the music. Say your intention out loud or silently in your mind.
4. Choose music that resonates with you and your spirituality. This may be a sacred chant, classical music, or soundscape.

Choose any genre of music that promotes a sense of peace and connection. It's often helpful to choose music without lyrics, as the words can distract you from your focus.

5. Close your eyes if this feels comfortable for you and tune in to your breath, breathing slowly and deeply, letting go of any tension in your body.

6. Tune in and focus on the music. Notice the different layers to the music, the instruments, the beat, and the rhythm. If your mind wanders, as it may well do, bring your focus back to the music and your breathing.

7. As you listen, pay attention to how the music affects your body.

8. Allow yourself to experience the emotions that arise; these may be joy, happiness, contentment, or feelings such as sadness, connectedness, or gratitude.

Nature Walks

A nature walk – whether a short 30-minute stroll or a longer, more challenging walk can be a powerful tool to connect with the Universe, enhance spirituality, and serve as a therapeutic exercise.

1. Before the walk, I want you to set an intention; this may be something like connecting with nature, seeking inner peace, or simply being present. Setting an intention for the walk can help to keep you focused and raise your awareness.

2. On the walk, use mindfulness to engage your senses fully; by this, I mean using your senses by paying attention to what you see, hear, smell and feel. Notice details like the textures of the trees, the sound of the rustling leaves, or the trickle of the brook.

3. Connect with the nature surrounding you and acknowledge life around you – from the trees to the animals – and

observe the sky and the earth beneath your feet. Going barefoot can help you feel more connected to the Earth, a practice known as grounding, believed to balance energy and improve well-being.

4. Practice gratitude for the natural world, thanking the Earth for all of the riches it provides us with, the beauty of nature, the warmth of the sun, and the changing seasons.

5. Reflect, focus on your breath, surroundings, and intention, and walk in silence to deepen your spiritual connection.

....

It saddens me to see so many people I work with in therapy living as if joy is scarce, seldom feeling the bliss of genuine connection. However, we can all tap into this daily. Part of developing healthy self-esteem is allowing yourself the time to invest in your spiritual growth, whatever that looks like for you as an individual. You may find it helpful to engage in different spiritual practices and see how they feel for you.

WAYS TO CONNECT WITH YOUR HIGHER SELF

We've looked at developing your own spiritual practice, but now I want to explore some other practical ways in which you can connect with your higher self.

Follow Your Heart's Desires

I want you to reflect now on what truly resides in your heart. Connect with this, for this is your higher self working within you. Connect with your true self, cease the constant striving and pushing for more, and, instead, embrace the belief that you are destined for more. This isn't just about material wealth; it's about transcending your physical self and tapping into the infinite abundance of the Universe, the Source from which we all originated. Recognize your inherent worth and know that you are deserving of all that your heart yearns for. Trust in this, for it is your birthright.

When we live from our higher self, we live from a place of innate knowing and intuition that this is our path. We start to live a heart-led life, which means following the whispers of our hearts. In order to tap into our intuition, we have to allow the space. For me, I know when my intuition speaks to me, as I feel it gutturally inside me and a sense of tugging at my heart. Be aware of the bodily sensations that you feel when you have an inner knowing, because this is your intuition speaking. To tap into this more often, allow yourself empty space to think and reflect. Stop filling every spare second with a task or a phone scroll and, instead, use this time intentionally for reflection, journaling, or simply observing things such as the sky or nature around you. My most vibrant experiences with the higher self come when I pause and embrace stillness. When you're struggling with a problem in life or trying to work out your next steps, allow yourself the time and space to figure things out.

My journey to living from my higher self started when I broke free from the social conditioning that heavily influenced my life – the belief that we should get a secure job and work in that job until we retire – and started to listen to an inner guidance. I learned to trust in myself, follow my intuition, and dare to do things that I felt within my heart's desire. Today, I've created a life that gives me more flexibility to engage in the things that light me up. My life hasn't always been this way. I've had jobs that required me to be there at a set time and work set hours each week. But I decided this wasn't the life I wanted, so I embarked on my entrepreneurial journey in 2017, leaving my 9-to-5 employment and starting my own business. But not just any business – one that was aligned with my purpose to support people as a therapist and coach.

As I sit and write this, I'm in my garden with the sun gently warming my skin, knowing that if I hadn't listened to that inner guidance from my higher self – my intuition – I wouldn't be sitting here right now, crafting this book. I had to make that decision for myself, and you can do it too. Whatever you want to change about your circumstances, you have the power inside you to do so.

Align with Your Higher Purpose

Aligning with your highest self involves becoming attuned to your deepest passions, qualities, and greatest desires, which all match the values you uncovered in Step 4 (*see pages 100–104*). You live from a place of true meaning in your life and contribute to the world, making a positive difference through your actions and having a meaningful impact on those around you. It's also very closely connected to living as your authentic self, which we explored in Step 4.

Aligning with your higher purpose is about connecting with something greater than yourself; this higher power gives you direction and meaning in life and can enhance your well-being in many ways:

- **A sense of confidence**: Tapping into your higher purpose gives you an air of confidence, meaning, and direction in life.

- **Motivation and commitment:** When you're living from your higher self, your motivation is increased and it becomes easier to work toward your desired path when you're aligned with your goals.

- **Resilience:** A higher purpose can provide a source of strength and resilience in the face of adversity, helping you navigate life's twists and turns with more ease.

- **Increased well-being:** Living from your higher self often involves engaging in activities that lift your spirits, connect to your soul, and offer holistic benefits for your mind, body, and soul.

Tapping into Your Higher Purpose

It can feel daunting if you haven't yet tapped into your higher purpose, but – trust me – it's a fulfilling and enlightening journey that you won't regret. Here are some tips to help you explore and align with your higher purpose:

- **Ask yourself what your interests and passions are.** What activities make you lose track of time? What subjects excite you or do you find intriguing? Often, our passions and interests are connected to our higher purpose.

- **Consider your values and strengths.** Go back to the VITALS exercise you did on pages 100–104. What core values mean the most to you? What activities do you find you engage in with ease and enjoyment? What are your natural strengths? Tapping into these can guide you toward your higher purpose by aligning your natural talents, strengths, and abilities.

- **Invest in your self-development.** Devoting time to your development can be a game changer. Reading books, watching inspiring videos, or listening to podcasts can all help to ignite your passions. Hearing about others' journeys can give you hope and inspiration to pursue your calling.

- **Don't be scared to try new activities.** Engage in things you haven't done before and then reflect on what feels like a good, energetic fit for you. These insights can help you gain more clarity on your own journey toward genuine authenticity.

....

There is a well-known saying that 'Life takes on a new meaning when you invest yourself in others.' This resonated deeply with me when I embarked on my first degree to train as a social worker. I knew I'd been called to work with others to help them heal and become the best version of themselves. My innate knowing that this was the path to take came from the higher self; the part of me that doesn't rely on logic, and innately knew a way to make this possible. When I started my training as a social worker at the age of 26, I didn't think this was possible for me. I had a criminal record at the time from my early experiences of shoplifting. I didn't have A levels, as I'd studied a BTEC in fashion design. However, luckily for me, it was enough to start an Open University degree, and I had completed a couple of modules that, unbeknown to me at the time, would provide me with enough UCAS points to apply to a traditional university. I chose to apply only to the University of Nottingham, where I live. This university is part of the Russell Group, representing 24 leading UK universities. I didn't apply to other universities – I trusted my inner guidance to apply there and only there. I was open and honest in my application about my criminal record at the time. And I used my past downfalls to demonstrate an authentic, compelling reason for wanting to support other disadvantaged people.

From my own journey and my work with others, I see common themes of dormant emotions, a lack of connectedness, and deep self-loathing. But the criminal record, the past, the bullying, or the hurt you experienced can only hold you back if you decide to let them. The key to unlocking your higher self is nurturing the spiritual part of you and realizing that you are connected to a bigger Source. Think about what brings meaning to your life, your broader purpose, and what you're here to achieve. Who are you here to serve, help, and love?

Discover the Joy in Each Day

It may not always seem feasible to experience the world around us as a completely pleasurable experience each day. Of course, things like work, caring responsibilities, household chores, and financial struggles may appear like an overwhelming, unavoidable distraction. Still, we can choose to be fully present and liberated from the concerns and distractions of our daily lives, even if momentarily. Each day is truly a gift, if we let it be. This means finding time each day to cultivate this mindset and incorporate things into your daily life that can help you connect to your higher self. Practices such as mindfulness, exercise, and connecting with others are helpful tools to build into your daily routine.

For me, exercise gives me a little bit of joy each day – I always feel uplifted and happier after I've moved my body. This used to come from my ego wanting to look a certain way and maintain a certain weight when I was younger, but this wasn't in a healthy way. Now, I experience exercise as an act of gratitude toward my body, a way of looking after it, and thanking it for its amazing abilities. It's a well-known fact that exercise releases endorphins, which are natural chemicals in the body that can improve our mood. In turn, this can also lower our stress levels. I know that some of you may have health struggles that limit the activity you can do, but I encourage you to find ways of being active at a level that's suited to your capabilities. I choose to walk my daughter to and from school so that I can enjoy the peace and headspace of just walking by myself for a moment after she has gone to school for the day. On other mornings, I'll listen to an audiobook or podcast, which is always related to the self-development arena. Meditation is a key part of my routine, too. I choose to do this just before I go to sleep at night. It's what I discovered works best for me, but I encourage you to find your own joy.

Embrace the Law of Attraction and Manifesting

While I won't go into the Law of Attraction in much depth here, as that topic alone could fill an entire book, I want to touch on how metaphysical concepts like this can help us connect to our higher selves.

Learning about the Law of Attraction has been an integral part of my spiritual development in recent years and has played a significant role in me writing this book. I love the teachings derived from the Law of Attraction. They've helped me manifest many positive things I never thought possible. I've manifested publishing this book, finding the support I needed in my business, opening a new outdoor office, and connecting with like-minded, inspiring women at a time when I needed them to appear in my life. When I started to tap into the whispers of God – the messages, signs, and synchronicities – things began to flow in my life in a way I had never known.

The Law of Attraction simply states that you'll attract whatever you focus on in your life. Whatever you give your energy and attention to, it will come back to you. It makes sense that if we experience low self-esteem and don't think highly of ourselves, we won't feel deserving or worthy of having more in our lives. As a result, we make choices that confirm that outcome for us. We settle for relationships that may not be healthy for us, or careers or jobs in which we don't feel fulfilled. In other words, we attract what we feel we're worthy of. As we grow in self-esteem and feel worthy and deserving, we automatically attract more positive things into our lives.

We must consciously connect with how our thoughts manifest in our lives. Healthy self-esteem facilitates access to our higher power, leading to a sense of ease in life and the ability to reach our full potential. When we tap into the energy of abundance and believe in ourselves, this nurtures our spiritual development. We feel aligned with the abundant nature within us and can more easily connect with something greater than ourselves. When living from the higher self, we understand how powerful we are in creating the lives we want. By trusting ourselves and our abilities, we accept responsibility for realizing our desires and we feel confident, supported, and motivated.

Upon reflection, I can now see that I've always been manifesting things in my life, though I wasn't consciously aware of this. Today, I'm much more open to metaphysical concepts and how they can support us in our spiritual journey, and have seen how they can help the clients I support, too. At the core of manifestation is using the power of positive thinking and aligning with the inner knowing and belief that what you want to attract in your life is possible. Because manifestation is all about harnessing the power of our minds, underpinned by the belief that our thoughts impact our reality, we can attract more wealth, happiness, and abundance into our lives when we believe that we're made for more and deserving of more.

Let's consider how you can harness the power of manifestation to reach your dreams, goals, and ambitions. Based on my own curiosity and practice, I have identified six key factors that enable us to become better at manifesting things in our lives:

1. **Set clear intentions.** It's crucial to be specific about what you want to unfold in your life. By setting clear intentions, we know what we want to achieve, which helps us focus on the said desire. Whether it's finding love, reaching a career or business goal, or attaining inner peace, you need to be specific and unwavering in your desires.

2. **Visualize your dreams.** Each thing I have manifested in my life first began with a thought. This is why our thoughts are so important. I love to daydream, and this is a crucial element in the manifestation process of visualizing your desired life. Sometimes, people may not always be aligned with your visions and dreams, but that is OK because your dreams belong to you. So, don't be afraid to allow yourself to daydream and visualize what you want to call forth into your life.

3. **Practice gratitude.** We looked closely at gratitude in Step 3 when we explored rejecting old stories, but I want to mention it again here, because I've witnessed first-hand how clients who choose to take a few moments each day to reflect on the blessings in their lives improve their outlook, happiness, and well-being. This helps with the manifestation process, because it creates a sense of abundance within you. This then impacts your mindset, making you feel more capable of manifesting your desires. You can practice gratitude by writing in a journal at the end of every day or first thing in the morning. There are even some cool apps you can download. Use whichever time of day feels most powerful to you to do this.

4. **Say affirmations:** In each step, we've been using affirmations to retrain the subconscious mind and reprogram old negative ways of thinking, but they're also a powerful way to reinforce your beliefs and align your thoughts with your desires. Even if

you don't fully believe your own words at first, expressing them will help strengthen your conviction. Over time, that belief will become genuine.

5. **Take inspired action.** Manifestation is not simply about hoping that the things you desire will appear. It's something that always requires action. Inspired action refers to taking the necessary steps to bring about the desires of your heart. An inspired action involves taking steps toward your goals that are motivated by a deep sense of purpose, an unwavering passion, and an intuitive feeling within. One of the ways this can happen is by developing yourself through education, surrounding yourself with the connections and community you need, or starting a new project. What is crucial to this process is that each step brings you closer to your dreams.

6. **Release resistance.** One of the hardest things I know I've encountered, yet an absolute game changer, is letting go of our fears and recognizing how our self-limiting beliefs can hinder our ability to manifest things into reality. This is where we call upon the higher power within us. It's all about trusting in divine timing and remaining open to receiving your desires in unexpected ways. Trust me, since I've applied this principle and taken inspired actions to manifest my desires, things happen and appear at the right time for me. What I once doubted is now a real possibility.

One of the things that I've struggled with in the manifestation process is when my desires don't come into my life as soon as I'd like them to. Often, we encounter bumps in the road and plans that don't unfold as expected. However, it's important not to get too hung up on what hasn't appeared yet in your life and instead keep taking inspired action toward your goals. Close your eyes if this feels comfortable for you and imagine every element of the life you aim to achieve, including the sights, sounds, and emotions associated with it. Allow yourself to feel the emotions therein. If we maintain faith that things will manifest in their own time and accept that they may not happen exactly as envisioned, we can trust that a better outcome or an alternative path will emerge to guide us forward.

Ed's Story

Ed, 31, worked as a healthcare support worker for ten years. While he loved serving and supporting others, his job wasn't fulfilling him anymore. He realized he was staying in a job he disliked because he was afraid to take the leap into his true passion. After connecting with his higher self, he started to trust that he was made for more. He took some courageous steps, leaving behind the security of his 9-to-5 job to pursue his passion as a musician. He felt this aligned with his higher calling. He loved the joy he could bring to others when he played music and performed. He opened his own business and, within months, was getting regular work and doing something that he was passionate about. The most rewarding part was he was living in alignment with his true self, which filled him with joy, confidence, and fulfillment.

••••

I want to congratulate you on reaching the end of the final step. I hope you've now grasped the importance of awakening your higher self and its links with self-esteem. I want to leave you inspired to develop your spiritual practices, act on your intuition, and nurture your higher self – this is the key to doing and achieving things you never dreamed possible.

I firmly believe in the untapped potential within you and I am confident that, by reaching this final chapter, your belief system has shifted. You're beginning to realize that you're made for more. You will also know that you're worthy of everything your heart desires. When you connect with your higher self, you can break free from the confines of low self-esteem and live a life that brings you more happiness, wealth, and abundance. This higher self is not just a concept, but a profound aspect of your being that, when embraced, can lead to a transformative shift in your life.

THERAPEUTIC EXERCISES
Stream of Consciousness Journaling

For this exercise, I would like you to complete some writing from your stream of consciousness. By this, I mean writing down your thoughts without overthinking them. This form of journaling should feel natural and is a process of allowing yourself to be guided by your intuition and just letting the words flow onto the page. Some people prefer to put a time limit on this exercise, say 10 to 15 minutes, or you may prefer to write until you come to a natural end.

Here are some questions for you to explore and journal upon:

- What resonated most with you in this chapter about spirituality, and why?

- Did any part of the chapter challenge your current beliefs or perceptions? How so?

- How do you envision deepening your spiritual journey?

- If a higher power supports the flow of the Universe, describe how you're in flow with the Universe when you accept yourself for who you are.
- How are you less in flow with the Universe when you feel self-loathing and unhappiness with who you are?
- What is one thing you could do to strengthen your flow with the Universe today?

Daily Check-in with the Higher Self

This week and, if possible, every day going forward, I want you to set aside a little time for reflection each morning or night, whenever works best for you.

1. Answer this question: How can I honor my higher self today?
2. Write down this reflection if you like, or silently keep it within your mind's eye.
3. Reflect on how you showed up today living from your higher self. Who did you support? Who did you influence? What did you contribute to the world today?

Awakening the Higher Self Guided Meditation

1. Make yourself comfortable. Close your eyes if this feels comfortable for you and focus on your breath. As you focus on your breath, breathe in deeply and breathe out slowly. Stay like this for a few moments until you enter a deep state of relaxation.
2. Imagine a bright white light, so beautiful and pure, glowing just above your head. This is the light of your higher self – your true, pure essence. As you focus on this light, feel

its warmth, comfort, and power. It's growing brighter and brighter.

3. Visualize this light now entering the top of your body through the crown of your head. Feel it filling your mind with illuminating thoughts. Every thought and every idea releases any doubts or confusion you once had.

4. Allow this light to flow down to your shoulders, releasing any tension. The light is now illuminating your chest as it reaches the area of your heart, where you feel your heart expanding and opening to the abundance of love and possibility. You experience a sense of peace and connection. A feeling of joy and love fills every bone in your body. This love within you is your higher self, the ever-present constant in your life. Your higher self always wants the best for you and guides you through your intuition.

5. Your higher self is not a distant entity, but a part of you, always within reach. Whether you seek guidance, reassurance, or comfort, it's there for you. This connection isn't a one-time event, but a constant presence in your life, ready to support you whenever you need it.

6. As you conclude this meditation, carry a sense of love and comfort with you as you navigate your day. Remember, the power of your higher self is always within you.

7. Gently bring your awareness back to the present moment. Feel the support beneath you, the air around you. Wiggle your fingers and toes, bringing movement back into your body. When you're ready, slowly open your eyes if they were closed, but keep the love and comfort you've experienced close to your heart.

•••••••••••••••••

Affirm:
I am a powerful creator of my reality.
I embrace my highest self.

MY FINAL NOTE TO YOU

As someone who has personally experienced the profound impact of low self-esteem, I understand the challenges it can bring to your life and happiness. My own journey of overcoming this, much like yours, and the support I now provide to my clients as a therapist have inspired me to share this book with you. It was a calling from my soul to write this book, and I hope it's resonated with you.

In *Believe You're Made for More*, we've delved into the root causes of low self-esteem and its life-altering effects, and explored effective strategies to conquer it. The seven steps we've completed are theoretical and practical techniques that, when applied, can reframe negative-thinking patterns, reveal our true selves, and foster self-love and acceptance. Witnessing my clients undergo these steps in therapy, I've seen them make monumental shifts in their lives, achieving what they once deemed impossible – from career changes and starting a business, to finding true love.

I hope this book has also inspired you to embrace who you truly are and to believe you deserve an incredible life. Now you're ready to break free from self-doubt and step into your higher power. This book is only the start of the transformation. Building self-esteem is an ongoing process and, as I mentioned at the start of this book, you can revisit any of the steps whenever you need to focus on a particular part of your self-esteem journey. You have my unwavering support every step of the way – so come and join me and my community at www.natashapagemsc.com.

Thank you for taking this journey with me. Your commitment to improving your self-esteem is commendable, and I am honored to have been a part of your growth. I'll leave you with one final exercise:

Creating a Higher Self Vision Board

You've come a long way on this journey – you have amplified your awareness, interrogated the old narrative you told yourself, rejected these stories, uncovered your authentic self, developed your self-acceptance, and embraced progression. Each day, you are connecting more and more with the most authentic version of yourself. I believe in your innate power and the highest version of you that is about to be birthed.

I now want you to envisage living from your higher self. What is the ripple effect you will cause when you live from this place? Your higher self transcends the ego and desires to create a positive impact on others around you. It strives to spread love and light to all of those who encounter you.

Stage 1: Create the Space

Allow yourself the time to create a calm space where you won't be interrupted. Create ambiance by lighting a candle and playing calm music. Breathe deeply and settle into the space you have curated.

Stage 2: Visualize Your Higher Self

Now, close your eyes if this feels comfortable for you, tap into your breath, and imagine standing in front of your higher self. This is the version of you that is purely authentic, unleashing your full potential.

- How do you stand?
- What is your posture like?
- What energy or presence do you exude?
- What kind of expression are you wearing? Confident? Joyful? Compassionate?
- What are you wearing? Is there a particular color or style that represents your energy?
- What does your higher self say to you as you look at them?

Take your time with this. Notice and write down every detail.

Stage 3: Step into Your Higher Self

Now, imagine merging with this version of yourself. As you step forward, feel the energy of your higher self becoming your energy. Feel the confidence, the love, the sense of purpose filling you up. Know that this isn't someone outside of you; this is you.

Stage 4: Journal or Vision Board Your Experience

When you're ready, I want you to create a journal or a higher-self vision board, merging both images and words to describe what this experience was like. You can use cuttings from magazines or your own art materials to form this vision. You can use words or just images – whatever you feel drawn to. You may want to consider what your higher self looks like, what it felt like to step into this part of yourself, and what actions you'll take in your life to live from this place from now on.

You are no longer someone striving to be more – you are more; you just need to believe it. You are your higher self and this part of you is emerging each day into the truest and most aligned version of *you*. Remember this exercise or look at your vision board whenever you need a reminder of the innate power within. If you ever feel a disconnect from your purpose, return to this vision of your higher self. Remember, your higher self is not separate to you, it is part of you; it is always within.

....

'Believe in yourself and all that you are. Know that there is something inside you that is greater than any obstacle.'

– Christian D. Larson

FURTHER READING

BOOKS AND JOURNAL ARTICLES

Ainsworth, M. D. S. and Bell, S. M. (1970), 'Attachment, Exploration, and Separation: Illustrated by the Behavior of One-year-olds in a Strange Situation,' *Child Development*, 41: 49–67.

Bowlby, J. (1953), *Child Care and the Growth of Love*. London: Penguin.

Bradshaw, J. (1999), *Home Coming: Reclaiming and Championing Your Inner Child*. London: Piatkus.

Dyer, W. (2019), *Happiness Is the Way*. Carlsbad, C.A.: Hay House Inc.

Elkins, D. N., et al. (1988), 'Toward a Humanistic–Phenomenological Spirituality,' *Journal of Humanistic Psychology*, 29(4): 5–18.

Fennel, M. (2016), *Overcoming Low Self-Esteem: A Self-Help Guide Using Cognitive Behavioral Techniques*. London: Robinson.

Ferrari, J. R. (2000), 'Procrastination and Attention: Factor Analysis of Attention Deficit, Boredomness, Intelligence, Self-Esteem, and Task Delay Frequencies,' *Journal of Social Behavior & Personality* 15: 185–96.

Freud, S. (1923), *The Ego and the Id* in *The Standard Edition of the Complete Psychological Works of Sigmund Freud*., Vol. XIX, pp. 1–66:

www.sas.upenn.edu/~cavitch/pdf-library/Freud_SE_Ego_Id_complete.pdf [Accessed May 13, 2025].

Gerhardt, S. (2024), *Why Love Matters: How Affection Shapes a Baby's Brain*. London: Routledge.

Gilbert, P. (2010), *The Compassionate Mind (Compassion Focussed Therapy)*. London: Constable.

Griffin, B. J., et al. (2017), 'Self-Directed Intervention to Promote Self-forgiveness,' in: L. Woodyatt, et al. (eds.), *Handbook of the Psychology of Self-Forgiveness*. New York: Springer, pp. 207–218.

Hay, L. (1994), *You Can Heal Your Life*. London: Hay House.

Lapsley, D. K. and Ste, P. C. (2012), 'Id, Ego, and Superego,' in: *Encyclopedia of Human Behavior*: www.researchgate.net/publication/237306175_Id_Ego_and_Superego [Accessed August 7, 2025].

Jeffers, S. (1987), *Feel the Fear and Do It Anyway*. New York: Ballantine Books.

Jung, C. G. (1951), *Aion: Researches into the Phenomenology of the Self*, trans. R. F. C. Hull. Princeton N.J.: Princeton University Press.

Prochaska, J. O., and Norcross, J. C. (2007), *Systems of Psychotherapy: A Transtheoretical Analysis*. Oxford: Oxford University Press.

Rogers, C. R. (1961), *On Becoming a Person: A Therapist's View of Psychotherapy*. London: Houghton Mifflin.

Rosenberg, M. (1979), *Conceiving the Self*. London: Basic Books.

Rubin, G. (2015), *Better Than Before*. London: Crown.

Selig, M. (2009), *Changepower!: 37 Secrets to Habit Change Success*. London: Routledge.

Storr, A. (2001), 'Ego, Super-Ego, and Id,' in: *Freud: A Very Short Introduction*. Oxford: Oxford University Press.

ONLINE ARTICLES

Copley, L. (2024), 'Hierarchy of Needs: A 2024 Take on Maslow's Findings': https://positivepsychology.com/hierarchy-of-needs/ [Accessed September 2, 2024].

Hayes, S. (2024), 'The Power of Writing About Your Values': https://medium.com/@stevenchayes/the-power-of-writing-about-your-values-0d73b6bdf136 [Accessed March 11, 2025].

Langwell, S. (2022), 'Fact: 85% of Us Suffer From Low Self-Esteem': https://medium.com/@shawnlangwell/fact-85-of-us-suffer-from-low-self-esteem-364cf613148 [Accessed February 17, 2025].

Medical News Today, 'Ways to Practice Shadow Work': www.medicalnewstoday.com/articles/what-is-shadow-work#ways-to-practice [Accessed September 2, 2024].

Nash, S. L. (2022), '10 Self-Affirmation Activities to Try': https://psychcentral.com/blog/self-affirmation-a-simple-exercise-that-actually-helps [Accessed September 2, 2024].

Psychology Today Staff, 'Neuroplasticity': www.psychologytoday.com/gb/basics/neuroplasticity [Accessed August 26, 2025].

Vivyan, C. (2010), *An Introductory Self-Help Course in Cognitive Behavior Therapy*: www.getselfhelp.co.uk [Accessed September 4, 2025].

Walcott, E. (2023), 'Rochelle Humes on Self-Care as Colgate's New Ambassador: "Be the best version of you"': www.standard.co.uk/showbiz/rochelle-humes-importance-selfcare-colgate-new-ambassador-be-ultra-campaign-b1054610.html [Accessed March 11, 2025].

BONUSES

Visit www.natashapagemsc.com for the following bonus resources:

- Access your **free downloadable *Believe You're Made for More* work booklet** featuring some of the exercises from the book.

- Listen to the **meditations in each step** as a free audio journey.

- Take the **online version of the Self-Esteem Questionnaire** on pages 8–9.

- Complete the **online version of 'How Ready Are You for Change?' quiz** on pages 172–176.

THANK YOUS

Writing this book was placed in my heart a long time ago. But it wasn't until the synchronicities aligned, guiding me on this path, that the journey truly began. I recognize that I couldn't have completed this book-writing journey alone. First and foremost, I offer my deepest gratitude to God, for it is through God's grace that this vision has come to fruition.

Mum and Dad, your unwavering presence in my life has been my anchor. Your resilience and hard work have been a constant source of inspiration, shaping me into the person I am today. I am deeply grateful for your sacrifices to provide for me, my siblings, Charlotte, Luke, and Ruth, and all six of your dear grandchildren, Chelsey, Thea, Emmanuel, Amelia, Jonah, and Olive. It's beautiful to see the values you embody reflected in all of us.

My beautiful husband, yes, it's a cliché, but you are indeed my rock; you support me and my ambitions, you live my ups and downs, and you genuinely are the most patient, loving, and caring husband. I am so full of gratitude to have you in my life. During the last 18 months, while this book was crafted, I've had to work tirelessly to get it completed; your support doesn't ever go unnoticed. I appreciate you so much and love you more than these words can express.

To my precious Chelsey and Thea – everything I do is for you. Your support through my book-writing journey means the world to me. Thanks for understanding and letting Mummy get on with her work. I cherish every moment we share as a family and want you to know that I love you both immensely.

Hay House, thank you. Firstly, I would like to thank the late Louise Hay. Upon hearing how Louise started Hay House, her inspiring story, and how she supported others, I knew Hay House was the publisher I was to work with. Michelle Pilley, the first day I saw you on stage at the Hay House Writers Workshop, I felt I could see into your soul, your face full of emotion. I felt drawn to your spirit; I could see how much it meant to you to have the aspiring authors in the room, and this was further confirmation that my book was to be published by Hay House. No journey is completely smooth sailing. My first book submission wasn't quite right, but you gave me a chance to resubmit, improve the concepts within my book, and make it the best it could be for the reader. Thank you for believing in my book, believing in me, and helping me grow and develop as an author. Kezia Bayard-White, I couldn't have asked for a better editor than you. I have embraced every minute of this book-writing journey, and your support, feedback, and monthly meetings kept me motivated and on track again. Thank you for believing in me. Julia Kellaway and Cathy Levy, your support in the last stage of edits and helping me get the book into the best possible shape was invaluable.

My mentors, Jessica Huie and Yamile Yemoonyah, your support and guidance were crucial in helping me shape that initial book proposal. I sincerely thank you.

Thank Yous

Sasha Archer, Zoe Fox, Kreena Dhiman, and Lindsey Van Wagner, as you embrace your book-writing journeys, I am so grateful to have met you and built friendships with you all. I can't wait to read your books.

To my dearest lifelong friends, Caroline, Becca, and Danielle – you've been by my side through every twist and turn of my journey.

Last but certainly not least, my valued clients, thank you for your trust in me; each of you has been instrumental in this journey. Thank you for allowing me to support you and inspire the insights that shaped this book.

My hope for this book is that it will have a lasting impact; it will help millions of people to realize their worth and believe they're made for more.

With love, Natasha x

ABOUT THE AUTHOR

Natasha Page is a highly respected psychotherapist, self-development and business coach, with over a decade of experience in helping individuals transform their lives. She is the creator of My Little Therapy Box – a resource designed to help people communicate more effectively about their mental health. A sought-after trainer, consultant, and speaker, Natasha regularly shares her expertise in the media and her work has been featured in Radio 4's *Woman's Hour*, ITV News, the BBC, *Psychologies* magazine, and the *Guardian*. She is also an agony aunt for *Pick Me Up* magazine and a BACP (British Association for Counseling and Psychotherapy) media spokesperson.

Natasha's mission is to empower people to recognize their inherent worth and capabilities and live their best lives, filled with purpose, success, and fulfillment. Whether through one-on-one sessions, group workshops, or her impactful writing, Natasha is committed to helping others achieve new heights of personal, professional, and entrepreneurial success.

Follow Natasha on her popular social media platforms for a regular dose of inspiration and valuable content.

@natashapagemsc
www.natashapagemsc.com

We hope you enjoyed this Hay House book. If you'd like to receive our online catalogue featuring additional information on Hay House books and products, please contact:

Hay House UK Ltd
1st Floor, Crawford Corner,
91–93 Baker Street, London W1U 6QQ
Tel: +44 (0)20 3927 7290; www.hayhouse.co.uk

Published in the United States of America by:
Hay House LLC
PO Box 5100, Carlsbad, CA 92018-5100
Tel: (760) 431-7695 or (800) 654-5126
www.hayhouse.com

Published in Australia by:
Hay House Australia Publishing Pty Ltd
18/36 Ralph St., Alexandria NSW 2015
Tel: +61 (02) 9669 4299
www.hayhouse.com.au

Published in India by:
Hay House Publishers (India) Pvt Ltd
Muskaan Complex, Plot No. 3,
B-2, Vasant Kunj, New Delhi 110 070
Tel: +91 11 41761620
www.hayhouse.co.in

Let Your Soul Grow

Experience life-changing transformation – one video at a time – with guidance from the world's leading experts.

www.healyourlifeplus.com

TRANSFORM YOUR DAY—ANYTIME, ANYWHERE

With the **Empower You** *Unlimited Audio App*

❝ ★★★★★ **Life changing.**
My fav app on my entire phone, hands down! – Gigi ❞

Unlimited access to the entire Hay House audio library!

You'll get:

- 600+ soul-stirring **audiobooks** to expand your mind
- 1,000+ **meditations** for restful sleep, morning focus, and gentle healing
- Bite-sized audios **under 20 minutes**—perfect for busy days
- **Exclusive talks** you won't find anywhere else
- **Daily affirmations**
- Fresh content added **every week** to fuel your journey

Listen to the audio version of this book!

❝ Driving, yard work, and housework have been **transformed**! – Ruffles27 ❞

Scan the QR code to start listening or visit **hayhouse.com/unlimited**

CONNECT WITH
HAY HOUSE
ONLINE

🌐 hayhouse.co.uk
📷 @hayhouseuk
🎵 @hayhouseuk

f @hayhouse
🦋 @hayhouseuk.bsky.social
▶ @HayHousePresents

Find out all about our latest books & card decks • Be the first to know about exclusive discounts • Interact with our authors in live broadcasts • Celebrate the cycle of the seasons with us • Watch free videos from your favourite authors • Connect with like-minded souls

'The gateways to wisdom and knowledge are always open.'

Louise Hay